JACQUELINE KENNEDY

A
WOMAN
FOR THE
WORLD

⚜ ⚜ ⚜

JACQUELINE KENNEDY

A
WOMAN
FOR THE
WORLD

⚜

BY ROBERT T. HARDING AND A. L. HOLMES

ALL PHOTOS FROM UNITED PRESS INTERNATIONAL

ENCYCLOPEDIA ENTERPRISES, INC.
NEW YORK

PREFACE

❦

"AND JUST AS I turned and looked at him, I could see a piece of his skull and I remember it was flesh colored. I remember thinking he just looked as if he had a slight headache. . . . He . . . put his hand to his forehead, and fell into my lap. . . .

"I used to think that if I had only been looking to the right, I might have seen the first shot hit him, then I could have pulled him down, and the second shot would not have hit him. . . ."

In these words, Jacqueline Bouvier Kennedy described to the Warren Commission the tragedy that was, in the drawing of a trigger, to mark her forever apart.

In her three years in the White House, Mrs. Kennedy had already become a cynosure. From every corner of the earth, from those in high and low places, had come adulation for her charm, her beauty, her intelligence and achievement. It had come from Canada to South America, from all of Europe to the far lands of the east. Everywhere, she had represented the best this country had to offer.

On November 22, 1963, out of the abyss of grief and an infinitude of dignity, Jacqueline Kennedy became another kind of symbol.

In this book we see how Jacqueline Kennedy's life prepared her for the role she was to play—a life in few ways typical of that of the American woman, but so typifying what women would like to be that she truly represents their aspirations.

❦

Mrs. Kennedy on ski vacation in Gstaad, Switzerland, during early part of 1966.

EARLY YEARS

❧

The circumstances of birth are, for the baby, pure happenstance. How gloriously fortunate, then, was Jacqueline Lee Bouvier on June 28, 1929.

A year before, Janet Lee had married John Vernou Bouvier III at St. Philomena's Church in East Hampton, Long Island. The bride was just twenty years of age, slim and very beautiful; the groom was dark and astonishingly handsome.

Some five hundred guests attended their wedding reception under a bright July sun on the lawn of the Lee home. After a honeymoon abroad, the couple returned briefly to Long Island and then moved to a duplex apartment on Manhattan's Park Avenue. They were young, wealthy, and in love. Their union had much to offer a child.

The child, however, seemed somewhat reluctant to accept. Birth had been planned to take place in New York and was expected in mid-May. Jacqueline arrived in Long Island, six weeks late and understandably chubby, weighing eight pounds. Awaiting her with varying degrees of impatience were numerous relatives, including a full complement of grandparents. If none was overwhelmed with her beauty at birth, it was of no matter. Simply by being, Jacqueline was somebody. She was, after all, a Bouvier.

The name, obviously, is French, and it came to this country first when André Bouvier, a youth of twenty-one from Grenoble, fought under Lafayette in the Revolutionary War. He was present at Yorktown when Cornwallis surrendered to Washington, but then returned to France. In 1815, his son Michel arrived in Philadelphia and went into importing and manufacturing, thus founding the family fortune.

Michel's business ability was passed on to his sons—Michel, Jr., and the first John Bouvier. Both made their mark at relatively early ages on the New York Stock Exchange. John married Caroline Ewing, who in 1869 founded the New York Foundling Hospital.

Their son, John, Jr., Jacqueline's grandfather, turned the family talents—of which he had more than his share, having been graduated Phi Beta Kappa from Columbia at twenty—to law. He had a brilliant career as an attorney and then, when past sixty, joined his uncle's brokerage firm. Besides success, the Bouviers all were blessed with longevity.

Mr. and Mrs. John V. Bouvier and their daughter, Jacqueline, attend horse show at Southampton Riding and Hunt Club, 1934.

8

Jackie, at 5, assisted by father, competes in horse show.

Jack Bouvier also went into Wall Street (after Yale), joining his great-uncle's firm. For a long time, however, it seemed that his principal career would be that of a bachelor. He was not simply good-looking, but strikingly so, with a strong resemblance to Clark Gable. Then, in his mid-thirties, he met Janet Lee.

She was sixteen years his junior. But she was *the* girl. She came from a family of comparable wealth (real estate and banking); she was intelligent; she was a delicately beautiful brunette. And she was an extremely gifted horsewoman, well on her way to the top of a sport that demands grace, discipline, and courage. Jack Bouvier was not particularly keen on riding, but he did admire the skill of the equestrienne. His bachelor days were over.

Jacqueline's first days were quite naturally filled with pets — in Bouvier terms, dogs and horses. Her first appearance in a show ring was at two, "handling" a black Scotty at East Hampton. This was duly recorded in the press, and so was her second birthday party, at which twenty small guests collided with "fistfuls of ice cream and cake." In the world of Bouviers and Lees, even the tots were newsworthy.

Jacqueline clearly was an exceptional child. She could talk at one, read surprisingly well at six, and was an accomplished horsewoman at the age of five. By this time, she was a child of eye-catching beauty. Story has it, however, that her deportment was something else.

"Mischief" is the word associated with her young years. It took many forms, from running away from her nurse in Central Park to teasing her younger (by three years) sister Lee, to "acting up" in school. This habit appeared to be developing into a disturbing pattern of rebellion at Miss Chapin's, an exclusive private school for girls in New York. Indeed, Jacqueline seemed to require discipline almost every day, until the headmistress, Miss Ethel Stringfellow, applied some sound psychology. Appealing to the child's love of horses, Miss Stringfellow pointed out

9

that even thoroughbreds must be schooled before they can perform. The message hit home. Jacqueline not only measured up to, she soon surpassed, the achievement level of her age group.

But for several years, all had not been quite what it appeared to be in the Bouvier household. When Jacqueline was eleven years old, her parents separated. Six months later, Janet Bouvier divorced her husband, and Jacqueline, who adored her father, now saw him only on Sundays. Despite the fullness of her life, it was a day for which she lived.

Jack Bouvier was good to his daughters. He was more than that. He was fun, too. On visiting days, he would borrow a dog from a pet shop for the girls to play with. Or he might take them to the movies or, occasionally, the racetrack. Later, when Jacqueline began attending Miss Porter's private boarding school at Farmington, Connecticut, he would treat her and her roommates to enormous dinners with no limit on desserts.

At the school, students were permitted to have their own horses. The cost of this, however, was something Jacqueline's parents felt unjustified, so she appealed to her grandfather, John Bouvier, Jr. He did not hesitate to furnish the sum of $25 a month, taking care to explain that, although he thought it an extravagance, he would do it to bolster her spirits.

With other college students, Jacqueline sails on French Liner to study at Sorbonne.

Senator John F. Kennedy with fiancee, Jacqueline Bouvier.

It was at this time—Jacqueline was fifteen—that her grandfather began playing a larger role in her life. He was past seventy years of age, but he corresponded regularly with his bright young granddaughter. His letters were so wonderfully elaborate in style, one can't help but feel they reflected the unusual mental gifts of the recipient as well as the sender. They contained a high degree of warmth and charm, but were hardly the fare one would normally offer a teen-age girl. But John Bouvier, Jr. was not about to write down to anyone.

Schoolwork presented a challenge, but it was never a burden. Jacqueline always had time for fun, sometimes reverting to the mischievous pranks of her days at Miss Chapin's. She was, however, a girl in firm control of her emotions.

Just prior to Jacqueline's entering Miss Porter's School, Janet Bouvier had married Hugh D. Auchincloss, a former lawyer who had established his own brokerage firm in Washington, D. C. He had three children, two sons and a daughter, by two previous marriages, and he and Janet would have two, a boy and a girl, of their own. The experience was new for the Bouvier girls, but it proved rewarding.

11

Hugh Auchincloss did not try to rival Jack Bouvier for the girls' affections. His ancestry was Scottish, his manner calm. They called him "Uncle Hugh," and he played the role with apparently more than passing success. He gave the girls two new homes, one in Virginia on the Potomac, another at Newport, Rhode Island. They were both happy homes.

If adjustments had to be made, Jacqueline apparently was making them quite well. Her school marks were consistently high, her attitude good. When her half-sister, Janet, was born, she wrote a poem to celebrate the occasion, predicting that Janet would be the first woman president of the United States. Two years later, her half-brother, Jamie, was born. It was an event of double importance to Jacqueline because his christening was coupled with her coming-out party at Newport.

Jacqueline was seventeen then, and she was an extraordinary young lady. She was named Debutante of the Year for her beauty, intelligence, and poise. That fall she entered Vassar.

College can be a trying experience for many young people, but Jacqueline encountered no such difficulty. She was a brilliant, sensitive student. Living away from home was not strange to her, nor, for that matter, was travel. Indeed, she seemed to thrive on the latter, hopping off for weekends at schools such as Yale and Harvard, and sailing to Europe at the conclusion of her freshman year.

Her first trip included a Buckingham Palace garden party, but the real high point was Paris. She loved it. And so, after her sophomore year, she arranged for a period of study at the Sorbonne. During this time she lived with a French family. It was a new experience for her; she lived not in luxury but in rather pedestrian circumstances.

The Comtesse de Renty was a widow, a survivor of a German concentration camp, where she had lost her husband. She had a small income and supplemented it by taking in students. Two other American girls had rooms with the Comtesse, whose household also included two daughters, one of them a divorcée with a four-year-old son. Only French was spoken.

The plumbing was primitive, the heat all but nonexistent. But Jacqueline took it in stride, even though she often did her homework in mittens. With one of the Comtesse's daughters, she toured Austria and Germany, traveling third class and enjoying every minute of it.

After a year, she returned home and entered George Washington University to complete her studies. At this time, she was persuaded to enter a *Vogue* Magazine contest that was offering to the winner a six-month job on the Paris edition. It was no easy competition, requiring a personal profile, a complete layout for an entire issue of the magazine, and an essay of some five hundred words on "People I Wish I Had Known." Jacqueline Bouvier took the prize, principally because her choice of people staggered the judges.

They were: Serge Diaghileff, the Russian ballet impressario; French poet Charles Baudelaire; and Oscar Wilde, the British author. Her reasons for her selections also impressed the judges.

"Baudelaire and Wilde," she wrote, "were both rich men's sons who lived like dandies, ran through what they had, and died in extreme poverty. Both were poets and idealists who could paint sinfulness with honesty and still believe in something higher. . . . Diaghileff possessed what is rarer than artistic genius in any one field, the sensitivity to take the best of each man and incorporate it into a masterpiece all the more precious because it lives only in the minds of those who have seen it and disintegrates as soon as he is gone."

Despite the effort and thought she had put into the contest, Jacqueline, at her parents' request, turned down the prize, choosing instead to visit Ireland with her step-brother, Hugh, Jr., whom she affectionately called Yusha. The following summer she toured Europe with her sister, Lee, driving from Paris to Spain and on to Italy. Then she came home.

Her preparation for what lay ahead was finished; she was twenty-two years old and ready for work.

⚜

ADULT YEARS

Jacqueline Bouvier's interests had never been of the everyday world. They were special affections, peculiar really to the life into which she had been born—horse shows, the arts, summer homes, winter homes, and travel abroad. She was a special product from a very special, and privileged, environment. However, she was by no means a dilettante and was, in fact, not satisfied to be simply a leader of society.

John F. Kennedy and Jacqueline Bouvier on lawn of the Senator's Hyannis Port home.

Massachusetts Senator John F. Kennedy announces he will not accept the vice-presidential nomination "under any conditions."

Washington Times Herald *inquiring photographer, Jacqueline Bouvier, photographs lady feeding goldfish in rooftop cooling pool.*

It is not strange then that she wanted to work. Her first (and, as it turned out, only) job was on a newspaper, the Washington *Times Herald*—at $42.50 a week. Family influence may have helped her—though it is difficult to imagine any newspaper turning down a girl of such caliber at that salary—but Jacqueline's determination was the decisive factor. The only job open on the *Herald's* editorial staff was that of "inquiring cameraman." Among newsmen, it is not considered a position of any particular prestige, but to Jacqueline, or to any youngster eager to work in a newsroom, it could not help but offer the marvelous excitement of challenge and opportunity. Jacqueline was so elated at its promise that she accepted it at once.

The intricacies of a bulky Graflex news camera would stump many men in the editorial offices of today's major newspapers, but Jacqueline solved them quickly by seeking out, and paying for, some intensive instruction. Then she went about her task of asking people

16

Tonight.
Cooler
row.

reau Forecast
11 a.m.

m.;
n.; 5:11 p.m.
Details. on Page 2

The Evening Bu

PROVIDENCE, RHODE ISLAND, SATURDAY, SEPTEMBER 12, 19

18 PAGES

NO. 214

CHURCH BOUND: Hugh D. Auchincloss, her stepfather, escorts bride of Senator Kennedy.

—Associated Press Wirephoto

600 Clerics Labeled Reds, Probers Say

Communist Attempt to Infiltrate Catholic Church Also Reported

Washington — (AP) — secret charges that Comm successfully infiltrated Ame churches today were spre open files of a congressio vestigation.

One witness said 6 clergymen are "secret" of the Communist Party an to four thousand others are fellow-traveling category."

The House un-American ties committee, which will r its sessions late this year or in 1954, made public the de testimony yesterday.

It came from former Communist leaders h how the Reds, unal religion by frontal a from within to see with the aid of un and pawns.

One witness, Mani of New York, said n Reds themselves ex achieve the success h realized.

Another, Benjamin New York, testified filtration of the Me the Communists cessful."

A third, Josep of New York, column plan "ra Johnson was Communist from member of th Commission Party nationa 1934 or 1935 to of the party's from 1936 to U.S. Com to 1929 muni

Sen. John F. Kennedy Weds Miss Bouvier

Story-book wedding weather favored Miss Jacqueline Lee Bouvier in Newport this morning as she became the bride of U.S. Sen. John Fitzgerald Kennedy of Massachusetts in St. Mary's Roman Catholic Church.

The Most Rev. Richard J. Cushing, D.D., Archbishop of Boston, performed the 11 a.m. ceremony, biggest and most ful event of Newport's so

banking families, and is a granddaughter of James T. Lee of New York and the late Mrs. Lee, and of the late Mr. and Mrs. John V. Bouvier Jr. of New York.

Crowd Gathers

As the hour of the ceremony approached a crowd of onlookers gathered. By 10 a.m., 500 persons had lined Spring Street, and guests had begun to arrive. The crowd grew to 3,000 by the time the bride appeared, escorted by her stepfather, Hugh D. Auchincloss. The

Pro-French Official Shot

Tunisia Natio Serious' Gene:

Casablai New viole bled Fren tified as N riously wou a police insp

It was th assassinat sassinatic

Jacqueline Bouvier marries
John F. Kennedy, September, 1953.

Will ify ase

narge ch

— Senator d today he designed to justified in nce report abeled a "re-

the hearing e Senate in- mittee, which ot say when.

he made the esday because ut Communist he Army said erday that the ld sections of nade it obvious nct Communist

ny said. releas- ort disclosed in- g national de- meaning of the

report was de- y by the Army or disclosure. hoice but to go e it publicly." Mc-

mation that there wrong with expos- aganda," he said. going to hide any opaganda or Com- a label of 're-

aid the document, onditions behind the was "95 per cent ropaganda" and was r to 37 Army com- y in the Far East. e will report to his on what he con- a sizable number of nd things put out unist Party discipline" s indoctrination texts nce personnel.

mittee received tes- lay from a former , now working for epartment, who said United Nations is Communists for es- that they do use it o track of planning and ind the Iron Curtain. outner, re- ed by

Marriage in Newport on September 12, 1953, made the front page of The New York Times *the following day.*

questions, recording their answers to the questions—some topical, some serious, some frivolous—and snapping their pictures. Children were her favorite subjects, but she interviewed celebrities as well. Among them was Mrs. Richard M. Nixon. Another was John F. Kennedy, who was no stranger when she went to Capitol Hill and asked him what he thought of the pages who worked in the United States Senate. (His reply, typically humorous, was to the effect that he felt the country might sometimes benefit if the pages and the Senators switched positions.) John Kennedy and Jacqueline had been introduced years before at a wedding. She was barely a post-debutante, he a Congressman in his early thirties, and the meeting had no significance for either one.

Their next was more memorable. It took place at the home of Charles Bartlett, a Washington newsman, former beau of Jacqueline's, and a friend of John's. Recently married, the Bartletts invited six friends to their home one balmy June evening. The announced purpose of the gathering was dinner, but the actual intent was to match Jacqueline Bouvier and John Kennedy. What is more, the plan worked, or at least it seemed to.

John Kennedy suggested he see Jacqueline home that night. The invitation was informal, offered as they walked to her car. It was neither accepted nor rejected, because another admirer of Jacqueline's—one of longer standing—appeared on the scene. Congressman Kennedy excused himself. They would not meet again for many months.

Jacqueline had little time to regret the separation. Hers was a full life, and the rest of that summer of 1951 was spent touring Europe with her sister, Lee. Besides, another man was in her thoughts and, during the

Christmas holidays that year, she became engaged to John G. W. Husted, Jr., a graduate of Yale, beginning a career on Wall Street. Because he worked in New York, she in Washington, their time together was limited. They saw each other on weekends, but this was not enough to sustain the engagement. They parted as friends.

John Kennedy came back, a more or less "side door" return, into Jacqueline's life. They dated once in public—the Blue Room of the Shoreham Hotel in Washington—and then saw each other mostly in the company of friends, such as the Bartletts. If they saw each other at all.

The man of the house sees his young wife off as she leaves for a day of classes at the Georgetown University Foreign Service School.

Attending "April in Paris" ball at New York's Waldorf Astoria in 1958.

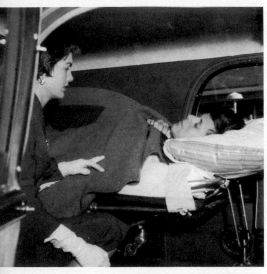

After near-fatal spinal operation in 1954, Senator Kennedy on his way to Florida.

Senator and Mrs. Kennedy with daughter, Caroline, at 18 months.

Kennedy was then making a bid for higher office, seeking the Senate seat held by Henry Cabot Lodge in Massachusetts. It was 1952, a very big Republican year, and Lodge, closely identified with the presidential candidate, Dwight D. Eisenhower, presented a formidable obstacle to a young Congressman. But Kennedy went after his goal with typical enthusiasm, remembering nonetheless to call Jacqueline from various points in the Bay State.

"It was a very spasmodic courtship," she said later. "He'd call me from some oyster bar up there with a great clinking of coins to ask me out the following Wednesday in Washington."

If it was an unusual courtship, it was an even more unusual election. Eisenhower swept the country by 6,000,000 votes, including a 200,000-vote plurality in Massachusetts. But John Kennedy, thirty-five-year-old three-time Congressman, won his Senate seat, in a stunning upset, by 70,000 votes.

The election over, Jacqueline saw more of John Kennedy. She would occasionally join him for lunch at the Capitol, spend an evening with friends playing bridge. The relationship was outwardly casual, and Kennedy was still described as one of the nation's most eligible bachelors. Indeed, when his proposal did come, their engagement announcement had to be delayed to avoid embarrassing a major magazine that had scheduled an article on his bachelorhood.

Despite the wealth in which they had grown up, Jacqueline Bouvier and John Kennedy were two quite different people. Her interests tended to be quiet, private ones; his were more vigorous and, since they centered around politics, almost boisterous by comparison.

Her temperament was independent, his competitive. One must compete in a group; one may be independent alone. But this difference, perhaps more than anything else, drew them together. If they had much to learn of each other, they also had an infinitude of good to offer each other.

Their courtship was interrupted quite suddenly in May of 1953 when, on two days' notice, Jacqueline was sent by her paper to attend the coronation of Queen Elizabeth II in London. The dispatches she sent back—newsy, humorous, "in" reports of the proceedings, parties, and ceremonies—made the front page, and so she was never far from the thoughts of John Kennedy—nor he from hers. She spent part of her time in London shopping for books he might enjoy, and when she flew home, the charges for excess baggage came to over $100.

When the plane touched down in this country, John Kennedy met Miss Bouvier at the airport. They became engaged within twenty-four hours. The announcement was made late in June, two days before her twenty-fourth birthday, and they were married three months later, on September 12, 1953, at St. Mary's Church in Newport, Rhode Island.

Sailing in the 32-foot Wianno Senior during a summer vacation in Hyannis Port.

It was a large wedding: ten bridesmaids in pale pink taffeta; fourteen ushers in formal dress; and three hundred guests. Richard Cardinal Cushing, then an archbishop, celebrated the nuptial mass and read a special Apostolic blessing. The day was bright and brisk. The reception was held at the Hammersmith Farm, her stepfather's home. Meyer Davis' orchestra played, as it had at the wedding of her parents and as it would at John Kennedy's inaugural ball. And if it all sounds like a fairy tale, in many ways it was. It continued through a honeymoon in Acapulco, where the couple rented a pink cottage perched high above the blue Pacific.

But their early years of marriage were to prove a trial for the young Kennedys. Within a year of their wedding date, John was on crutches. His back, injured first in football at Harvard, then aggravated severely during the war when his PT boat was sunk by a Japanese destroyer, had been operated on once before. But success was only partial, and, as the discomfort and pain increased, he agreed to another operation, entering the Hospital for Special Surgery in New York in October, 1953. The risk was great. Almost too great. Infection followed the operation, and

21

The Kennedys relax with daughter, Caroline, at their summer home in Hyannis Port.

one night his condition grew so critical that his family was summoned and last rites administered. But John Kennedy lived the night and eventually, after a six-week convalescence in Palm Springs, was strong enough for yet another operation! A long convalescence followed, but the time was not wasted.

In 1940, John Kennedy had written a best-selling book, *Why England Slept,* and now, during this enforced idleness, he began work on another, *Profiles in Courage,* a study of the political careers of eight men who put principle before convenience. It would win him a Pulitzer Prize.

Jacqueline personally selects fruits and vegetables for the Kennedy household.

Kennedy's back difficulties were not resolved satisfactorily until April of 1955, when he was referred to Dr. Janet Travell, who treated his muscular spasms with direct injections of novocaine. That year, Jacqueline also had need for a doctor. She suffered her first miscarriage.

Twelve months later, Jacqueline was to have still more difficulty. It was 1956, an election year, and Jacqueline, pregnant, accompanied her husband to Chicago, where he was to make a bid for the Democratic vice-presidential nomination. It was a hot, humid period, and Jacqueline spent most of the convention in a hotel room. It was not a happy time for

23

her, nor for Jack. He came within a few votes of gaining his prize, but then lost. Disappointed, he left for the Riviera.

Then the baby came—one month earlier than expected. It was a girl. Stillborn. Kennedy flew home to his wife, and if their spirits were low, their "tests," for a while, anyway, were over. The Kennedys were about to come upon brighter days.

They started in 1957. First came a Pulitzer Prize, and then Caroline was born, the day after Thanksgiving. This good fortune continued on into 1958, when John Kennedy was re-elected to the Senate by a record plurality of over 800,000 votes. It carried over into 1960.

Mrs. Kennedy smiles for photographers on the lawn of home, after a meeting between her husband and Adlai Stevenson.

24

Caroline receives instruction in painting from her mother.

Jacqueline was pregnant again that year. And her husband was seeking another nomination, this time for the presidency of the United States on the Democratic ticket.

Politics was not one of Jacqueline's favorite interests, and campaigning did not attract her greatly. She had, however, grown used to it. During her early years of marriage, she often accompanied her husband on speaking engagements around the country, and, in 1958, she made many trips to Massachusetts. She did not, however, attend the 1960 convention in Los Angeles but remained at Hyannis Port, Massachusetts.

In support of her husband's election, Jacqueline works on a weekly column called "Campaign Wife," distributed by the Democratic National Committee.

There, as the delegates cast the ballots that would decide her future as well as that of her family, she passed the time painting.

Her role in politics until then had been small, and there were some in her husband's party who felt she might be a hindrance. But they did not know her. Even so astute an observer as historian Arthur Schlesinger, Jr., admitted to being somewhat surprised when he first had an opportunity to talk with her at length.

"In the course of the evening," he wrote, "I realized that underneath a veil of lovely inconsequence, she concealed tremendous awareness, an all-seeing eye, and a ruthless judgment."

Now, as the wife of a national candidate, she came into public view, and it was soon apparent that her impact was going to be considerable. Martha Weinman put it this way in *The New York Times:* "When Jacqueline Kennedy, then five days the wife of the Presidential candidate, stepped aboard the family yacht in Hyannis Port, wearing an orange pullover sweater, shocking pink Capri pants and a bouffant hairdo that gamboled merrily in the breeze, even those newsmen present who could not tell shocking pink from Windsor rose, knew they were witnessing something of possible political consequences."

Indeed they were. She was, in fact, something rarely seen in a national political arena—a beautiful young woman with charm and intelligence.

She was at her best when called upon to address groups in languages other than English. Such an occasion arose on Columbus Day in New York, when Puerto Rican voters turned out enthusiastically to cheer John Fitzgerald Kennedy. But if he received a warm reception, it was "icicles in Greenland" compared to the thunderous outburst when Jacqueline stepped to the microphone and spoke to them in Spanish.

She contributed in other ways, such as writing a column somewhat quaintly titled "Campaign Wife," which was distributed to Kennedy campaign workers throughout the country.

On election day, she voted with her husband in Boston and then drove with him to Hyannis Port to await the results. It was a long, long wait. Early returns gave Kennedy a substantial lead from major cities, but then, as late returns came in, his lead dwindled. Kennedy urged his wife to retire early that night, and she did.

Nixon did not concede until the next morning.

Talking with mother, Mrs. Hugh D. Auchincloss, at McLean, Va., home during election-eve tea, in November, 1960.

During 1960 campaign, the Kennedys are showered with confetti and ticker tape at a tumultuous reception in New York.

At thirty-one, Jacqueline Kennedy was the wife of the thirty-fifth President of the United States and the First Lady of the land—a prospect that must prompt private thoughts. And on that morning, Jacqueline Kennedy, in an old raincoat, a simple kerchief tied around her head, walked the beach of Cape Cod . . . alone. She would rarely enjoy the luxury of solitude again.

FIRST LADY

The ceremony by which America transfers her leadership from one man to another is a simple one. There are speeches, parades, and prayers, but the actual change is effected by the administering of the oath of office. It consists of just thirty-five words.

President and Mrs. Kennedy entertain the Lyndon Johnsons at a White House dinner party.

Enjoying post-election solitude, Jacqueline walks alone on beach near Cape Cod home.

Painting by Mrs. Kennedy depicting nomination triumph of her husband.

John Fitzgerald Kennedy repeated those words a few minutes before one o'clock on the afternoon of January 20, 1961. It was bitterly cold, and his words came in puffs of frost. But when he delivered his inaugural address, hatless and coatless under a winter sun, he brought warmth and hope to millions of people on this earth.

"Let the word go forth," he said, "from this time and place . . . that the torch has been passed to a new generation of Americans—born in this century, tempered . . . disciplined . . . and proud of our ancient heritage. . . ."

It was a memorable address, spoken forcefully by the youngest man ever to be elected President. Its message was not lost on Jacqueline Kennedy. When the new President had finished, his wife's face was aglow. In the midst of thunderous applause and turmoil, she made a gesture rare for her in public—she touched her husband gently.

Now John and Jacqueline Kennedy became household words—the whole world knew them as Jack and Jackie.

Jacqueline Kennedy did not hesitate to hold high the torch of which her husband had spoken. The inaugural celebrations were hardly over when she began a monumental task—the restoration of the White House. It was a goal she had decided on shortly after the election.

A tour of the White House in mid-November had disappointed her greatly. There was a decided lack of pre-1900 furnishings, while those that did date to earlier days were haphazardly arranged, many pieces having no relevance at all to their settings. In short, the home that had housed every President save Washington seemed totally lacking in historical significance.

Other First Ladies had noticed this, among them Mrs. Calvin Coolidge. But, due to lack of funds or supporting enthusiasm, they were unable to effect any great change. Jackie decided to try.

Mrs. Mamie Eisenhower shakes hand of the future First Lady after taking her on tour of the White House.

John F. Kennedy is inaugurated as President of the United States.

Her first step was to order a number of books about the White House from the Library of Congress. These she studied while recovering at Palm Springs from the birth of her second child. When Inauguration Day came, she knew her plan well—to make the White House a living reflection of the times through which it, and the nation, had come, and to do so by relating all of its furnishings to those whose home it had once been.

It was an awesome task, but one for which Mrs. Kennedy was not unprepared. Although not a scholar of American history, and less than an expert on antiques, she had been trained by schooling, travel, and society to know and appreciate quality. She wanted only the best and most authentic furnishings for the White House and, most important, she knew how to go about getting them.

The job called for organization, so she set up three authorities—the White House Historical Association, the Committee of the Fine Arts Commission for the White House, and the Advisory Committee to the Fine Arts Committee. She persuaded Henry F. duPont, multimillionaire and founder of the famed Winterthur Museum of Americana in Wilmington, Delaware, to head the Fine Arts Committee and then enlisted leading directors and curators of museums and art galleries as members of the Advisory Committee. This put at her fingertips the most knowledgeable advice in the land.

The next problem was money. Mrs. Harry S. Truman had once redecorated the White House for $213,000, but Jackie's plans were so extensive that this would not even begin the job. Indeed, by the time she was through, the cost of the Green Room alone was greater than the entire amount spent by Mrs. Truman. Federal funds were not available on this large a scale, so Jackie urged Congress to designate the White House as a national museum, thus permitting it to receive gifts that would be tax deductible.

She then began her collecting, establishing something of a reputation among antique dealers as a hard bargainer. Once a desk or a painting or a rug had been selected, there was still the task of finding an individual, a corporation, or a foundation to pay for it. Many private citizens, hearing of her plans, donated specific items, and even offered to furnish entire rooms. In a short time, the value of gifts presented to the White House totaled more than $1,000,000.

Most of the donations were used to restore the four main rooms of the White House: the Green Room, the Red Room, the Blue Room, and the Diplomatic Reception Room.

As well as receiving contributions from outside the White House, Jackie discovered many treasures long forgotten by previous occupants. One of these was a desk made from the timbers of a British sailing ship, presented by Queen Victoria to President Rutherford B. Hayes. Jackie had it dusted off, and John Kennedy used it in his own office.

34

President and Mrs. Kennedy welcome Prince Rainier and Princess Grace, reigning monarchs of Monaco, to White House.

Vice President Lyndon Johnson
chats with Jacqueline
and the President at inaugural
ball in Washington on
January 20, 1961.
First Lady's gown is from
Bergdorf-Goodman.

With Madame Hervé
Alphand, French Ambas-
sador's wife, arriving for
reception in honor of Com-
édie Française.

37

Still another task remained. The White House is a home, an office building, and an official residence where guests of the nation are entertained. It is also a shrine of sorts and, as such, is open at specified times to the public. But tourists, both American and foreign, had no guidebook to tell them of the history of the building they were visiting, nor of its furnishings. Such a book, Jacqueline felt, was definitely needed.

After greeting Tunisian President and Mrs. Bourguiba at airport, First Couple leave for White House as he fixes her wind-blown hair.

Two of the world's most beautiful women, Princess Grace and Jacqueline Kennedy, meet at White House, May 24, 1961.

After taking helicopter from airport, Indian Prime Minister Jawaharlal Nehru walks with Mrs. Kennedy toward White House.

Mrs. Alan B. Shepard, Jr., wife of astronaut, visits White House.

First Lady welcomes Finnish President Kekkonen and wife.

Mrs. Kennedy attends dinner given by Japanese Prime Minister Hayato Ikeda in her honor. President was unable to attend due to illness. Vice President Johnson substituted.

Mrs. Kennedy welcomes renowned cellist, Pablo Casals.

Chancellor Konrad Adenauer poses on north portico of White House, prior to luncheon in his honor.

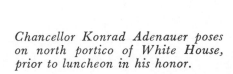

Few were enthusiastic about this project. Indeed, many thought it would be undignified to sell such a directory. But Mrs. Kennedy saw it not only as a convenience for those who had come so far to see the White House but as a means of raising funds that would ensure the continuity of the restoration. She had one published.

The results were staggering. More than 350,000 copies were sold in the first six months of publication, while the net profits at the end of the year amounted to more than a quarter of a million dollars. This not only delighted Jackie, it greatly pleased the President. He was impressed by the scope and efficiency of the job done by his wife.

Former President Truman helps First Lady remove cape as she takes place at Democratic Party's $100-a-plate fund-raising dinner marking first anniversary of inauguration.

First Lady, right, *presents gift to patient at Children's Hospital in Washington, D.C.*

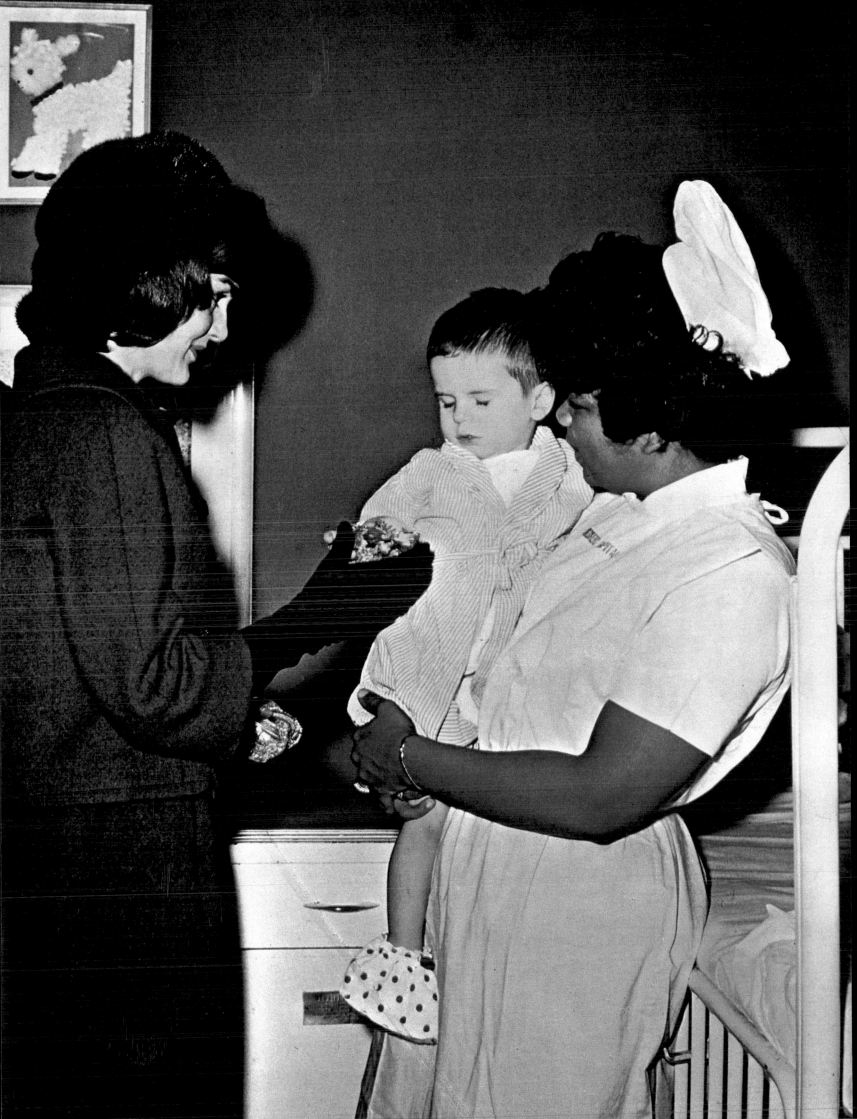

After reception honoring winners of the Nobel Prize in April, 1962, President and First Lady talk with novelist Pearl Buck and poet Robert Frost.

Famed composer-conductor, Igor Stravinsky, arrives for small, intimate dinner in his honor.

Opposite, *in whispered conversation with Secretary of State Dean Rusk.*

The nation at large had little knowledge of the changes until early in 1962, when Mrs. Kennedy conducted a tour of the White House for television. Though some critics commented on the "smallness" of her voice, the estimated nationwide audience numbered over forty-eight million. She had accomplished what she had set out to do, and the effectiveness of the restoration, the guidebook, and the telecast were such that the number of visitors to the White House jumped some sixty-six percent that year.

The building that housed America's First Family had been truly converted to America's First Home.

Had this been Jacqueline Kennedy's sole contribution to her husband's days in office, it still would have left a lasting mark. But a First Lady has many duties. So determined was she to make the White House and office of the Presidency a cultural as well as a political center—to show the world that America was an intellectual a swell as an economic force—that her duties and schedule became overwhelming.

She aided many causes, among them the establishment in Washington of a national cultural center for the performing arts (now known as the John F. Kennedy Center for the Performing Arts). In addition to lending her name and energies as co-chairman, along with Mrs. Eisenhower, she contributed two of her own paintings, which were ultimately made into Christmas cards and sold to aid the Center's fund drive.

Her main role, however, as wife of the President, was to serve as hostess for the nation. She created quite a stir in this capacity when, soon after entering the White House, she installed a French chef. It seemed an unnecessary, if not almost an un-American, gesture to many, but the complaints were few from White House guests.

It was even reported in the press that the cuisine was not only the best of its kind in Washington, but was superior to that of the French Embassy.

Jackie's talent for hospitality went far beyond satisfying the palate. On a weekday evening she might arrange an informal dinner for six or

Nation's largest polaris submarine, the Lafayette, is christened at General Dynamics shipyard in Groton, Conn., May 8, 1962.

Escorted to Newport, R. I., dinner by Australia's Ambassador to U.S., Sir Howard Beale.

47

eight stimulating people. As often as not, they were entirely unrelated to politics or government, host or hostess. Her purpose was to provide an atmosphere of vibrant relaxation and, from all reports, she succeeded magnificently.

Her official receptions were larger, grander, but no less stimulating. Guests found ash trays at hand (they had been removed by Mrs. Eisenhower), and cocktails and highballs were served before dinner. On one occasion, when the Kennedys held their first reception for members of Congress, the receiving line—a trial for both those who must stand and greet and those waiting to be greeted—was done away with.

It is interesting to note here the conflicts that arise for all who occupy the White House. On this very same evening in April, 1961, it

World's most famous work of art is unveiled at National Gallery. Standing on either side of painting are French Minister of Culture Malraux and wife.

President Mohammad Ayub Khan of Pakistan at Kennedy country estate, Glen Ora, in Middleburg, Va. First Lady rides Sardar, a gift of the Pakistani President when she visited his country during winter of 1962.

Water-skiing with Astronaut John Glenn when he and his wife were week-end guests of Kennedys in Hyannis Port.

Accompanied by John D. Rockefeller, III, Jackie arrives at Philharmonic Hall, New York City.

Family portrait with President's mother and father in November of 1960.

became evident that the landing of Cuban nationals at the Bay of Pigs was doomed to failure. The President kept abreast of developments throughout the night, withdrawing a number of times to discuss the situation with key aides. Decisions were made while the party continued. They were particularly difficult decisions for John Kennedy, for their chief effect was to remove all hope for a brave band of men fighting desperately for freedom. Yet only those involved in the decision-making process were aware of the emergency. So the ball went on.

If Jacqueline Kennedy held the title of Washington's leading hostess through courtesy, she established it in fact later that year when she arranged a state dinner for President Abboud of the Sudan. The food was superb, the music-filled atmosphere enchanting, the Shakespearian entertainment superior. Its significance was not lost on the intellectual community.

"I'd be willing to bet," noted one scholar, "that this is the first time Shakespeare has been performed inside the White House."

These dinners not only delighted foreign dignitaries, they dazzled Washington's jaded diplomatic set, to whom American official entertainment of such graciousness had not been generally known. Nor were the intellectuals of the land accustomed to finding themselves in the

Attending fashion show at U. S. State Department, advertised as "The Commonwealth Costume Cavalcade." Event was held for benefit of International Disaster Relief of American National Red Cross. Models were children from different nations of the world.

51

Mrs. Johnson is escorted to Old Supreme Court Chamber, where she was guest of honor at luncheon for Senate wives.

White House. In April of 1962, forty-nine Nobel Prize winners in art, literature, and science were invited to dinner. Jackie received one group of the guests in the Blue Room while her husband played host to the others in the State Dining Room. After the dinner, John Kennedy made his oft-quoted remark that such an assemblage was "the most extraordinary collection of talent, of human knowledge, that has ever been gathered at the White House, with the possible exception of the time when Thomas Jefferson dined alone."

John Kennedy's wit and quick intelligence, coupled with Jackie's elegance, created an aura of sparkling charm and warm dignity that had never been equaled in the White House. An invitation to dine at 1600 Pennsylvania Avenue was no longer a duty or even a simple honor. It was a coveted invitation to a splendid evening, one to enjoy, one to remember.

Jacqueline Kennedy also understood how to use entertainment to the advantage of the nation's image abroad. A luncheon for Premier and Mrs. Ikeda of Japan was unique in that former President and Mrs. Eisenhower were invited. What better evidence of America's brand of democracy than for the leaders of the two major political parties to jointly welcome a visitor from abroad?

Sketch of White House by First Lady was always kept on the President's desk.

Two Christmas cards painted by Mrs. Kennedy to be sold for the benefit of the National Cultural Center in Washington. "Gold Tidings," below, "Journey of the Magi."

When Lady Dorothy Macmillan, wife of the British Prime Minister, visited Washington, Jackie received her in the Oval Room, serving tea and small English cakes and sandwiches. President and Mrs. Kekkonen of Finland, entertained at luncheon in the State Dining Room, found blue and white flowers—the colors of their national flag—on the table, while the Marine Corps band played "Finlandia."

Many others were guests, including Emperor Haile Selassie of Ethiopia, the Shah and Empress of Iran, President Charles de Gaulle of France, and Chancellor Konrad Adenauer of West Germany. But Jackie's most memorable moment as a hostess was reserved for President Ayub Khan of Pakistan. It was also her most controversial moment, for the cost of the reception seemed excessive to many. Still, few who attended were willing to press the point. It was so memorable a night.

The site for this occasion was Mt. Vernon, the home of George Washington and a national shrine. It did not seem an inappropriate choice to Jackie, who had only recently returned from France, where she and the President had been entertained by President de Gaulle at Versailles. It had been a magnificent evening and especially so for the former Jacqueline Bouvier, who had a particular fondness for French history. To use the beauty and tradition of a nation's past for official functions seemed not only reasonable to her, but inspired. It had not been done before in Washington, but Jackie refused to be reined by tradition.

The setting was breathtaking. The grounds were sprayed with insect repellent; three generators were hauled from Washington to provide special lighting; butlers and security personnel were taken by bus from the White House, as were the chefs, food, silver, and china. The guests arrived by boat. Dinner was served on the lawn under a tent pavillion with a wood floor, specially carpeted in green.

The entire National Symphony Orchestra played throughout the evening. Nothing quite like it had been seen before in Washington. For one night, there was something spectacular, something special to a Washington reception.

Jacqueline Kennedy supplied that something. It was the same magic she applied to the restoration of the White House—a magic she cast over her every endeavor in her conscientious search for the best her country had to offer.

Arriving for dinner at the home of New York Herald Tribune *reporter,* Rowland Evans, Jr.

WIFE
AND
MOTHER

⚜

The demands on a young wife and mother in Jacqueline Kennedy's position are great. Although wealth eases her burden of household tasks, she is apt to find that position, duty, and fame are even more difficult to carry. Few women take it on willingly, because one must pay for the privilege in time and privacy lost. Mrs. Kennedy was no exception, but she assumed the responsibilities without complaint.

For her, a husband was someone with whom to share interests and experiences. She found this difficult when it came to politics, and especially resented criticism of John Kennedy. At such times, he would patiently explain to her that politics was not a subject to be taken personally, for one's foe today might be a much-needed friend tomorrow. Still, there were areas in which she could contribute to his career—she had begun finding them even before they were married. When Kennedy expressed interest in some French articles and books on Indo-China, she translated and summarized them for him. And, since American history was his favorite subject, she began taking courses in it soon after their marriage.

All this gave her greater understanding of his interests and, during his convalescence from back surgery, she found more ways of sharing them. An active, energetic man, Kennedy bitterly resented being confined to a bed. But when he began to think about writing, Jackie encouraged him by doing research, reading to him, organizing and taking down his notes. Her contributions did not go unrecognized, for, in the preface to *Profiles in Courage,* he wrote: "This book would not have been possible without the encouragement, assistance, and criticisms from the very beginning by my wife, Jacqueline, whose help during all the days of my convalescence I cannot ever adequately acknowledge."

Caroline plays with brother John, February, 1961.

The John F. Kennedy summer home at Hyannis Port.

Returning from vacation in Greece, Jacqueline is met by husband at National Airport.

On family farm in Middleburg, Virginia, Caroline takes a riding lesson from her mother as they await arrival of the President.

Jackie not only shared his enthusiasms but got him to share hers— among them, painting. He took to it with such zest that it created quite a laundry problem. Painting in bed, he frequently wielded the brush with such vigor that he got as much paint on the sheets as he did on the canvas. Once he was up and about, John Kennedy never went back to painting, but his work showed real promise.

But, though he gave up painting, Jackie saw to it that his interest in art was maintained. With some cleverness, she selected pictures that related to subjects he was particularly fond of, such as boats and sailing.

As a rule, she never questioned him about his work, nor did she try to interfere. Many say this was one of the reasons John Kennedy prized her so. But on at least one occasion she did press a point, and a sound one it was. During Kennedy's presidential years, plans were submitted for the reconstruction of Lafayette Square, facing the White House. A number of fine old houses were to be replaced by office buildings and, though John Kennedy himself did not relish the thought, there seemed no way to halt their demolition. Jackie, however, urged her husband to find another solution, even after the plans had been approved. And he did—the office structures were put up behind the graceful old landmarks, thus preserving an important part of Washington's history.

Time together was sorely limited. A good part of the early years of the Kennedys' marriage was spent campaigning, which meant extensive travel. After they moved into the White House, any time alone was a luxury. In fact, it had to be scheduled for the lunch hour or during a break in the President's busy afternoon. Jackie was important to the President in many ways, and, after a particularly trying event or decision, John Kennedy usually sought her advice. Such a time came after he delivered a television address at the height of the Cuban missile crisis. The consequences of his talk were highly problematical—at best, a lessening of tensions; at worst, nuclear war. That night the President dined alone with his wife.

She wanted it that way, too. According to Theodore Sorenson, the President asked her at that time whether she didn't want to be nearer the special underground shelter for the First Family. Her reply was direct; she stated that if an attack did come, she would come to his office and share the consequence.

Jacqueline Kennedy would have preferred more time with her husband. She felt very strongly about her home and wanted, in the real sense of the word, a family. Creating the atmosphere of a home took a great deal of effort, if only because she had so many homes to run.

The Kennedys bought their first in 1956 near Jacqueline's stepfather's "Merrywood" in Virginia. They were expecting their first child, and they purchased a large rambling house they called Hickory Hill. But, when the child was stillborn, they sold the house to Robert Kennedy and his rapidly expanding family.

Mother and children, November, 1961.

Kennedys arrive for mass at St. Francis Xavier Church in Hyannis.

Family on way to Hammersmith Farm in Newport, R. I. Right, eight-month-old John, Jr., in father's White House study.

Three weeks after Caroline was born, the Kennedys moved into a house on N Street, in Georgetown—a three-story, red brick, Federal-style building, the front door opening onto the sidewalk. It had a slight slant to it, but this gave it a personality that Jackie cherished. Behind it was a bricked courtyard with a magnolia tree.

In running that home, and the others to come, Jackie was something of a wonder. Her standards were firm, her taste impeccable, her attention to the more creative details astonishing to all who knew her. The result was an efficient, yet surprisingly comfortable, place in which to live.

But Georgetown was only one of their homes. The Kennedys also lived at Hyannis Port, Palm Beach, Virginia, and often visited at Newport or Camp David. And, of course, there was the White House. The problems of putting one's imprint on all these, and having that mark be one of distinction, is almost impossible to imagine. Yet Jacqueline Kennedy managed it, and more.

The responsibility of so many households did not interfere with what she considered her most important role—that of mother. She cared for her children with intelligence and deep love. She had had great difficulty bearing them, and would have even more before she left the White House. Her second son, Patrick, was another premature birth, another Caesarian, and another tragedy. It occurred in August of 1963, and, again, almost cost her her life. The baby lost his, after thirty-nine hours, due to a lung infection.

Mrs. Kennedy employed an experienced nurse for Caroline and John, but spent as much time with them as her schedule allowed. She would read to Caroline from a picture book on Louis XVI, and taught her to sit a horse at an early age. John seemed less interested in horses, but both children loved pets. By the time they left the White House, they had a staggering collection, including four dogs, two hamsters, two ponies, and assorted ducks.

A sense of humor helped her. She once told a broadcaster: "I always imagined I'd raise my children completely on my own. But once you have them, you find you need help. So I do need Dr. Spock a lot and I find it such a relief to know that other people's children are as bad as yours at the same age."

As a former reporter who had once interviewed the nieces of President Eisenhower, Jackie knew the risks that public life entailed and went to great pains to protect her children as best she could from publicity. But she also felt that they should take part in the life of the White House and often introduced them to visiting dignitaries. Once, during a ball, she spied Caroline and her nurse on the stairs and invited them down to join the party. Invariably, the children were well behaved, though John-John once had a bit of a tantrum when, at an official reception, someone failed to pass him the cookies.

Attracting attention of New York's Madison Avenue shoppers.

Caroline was permitted the run of the White House and accompanied her father to his office each day. In the evening, when the President took a swim in the White House pool, the children and Jackie often joined him. And, at bedtime, regardless of what event was planned for the evening, Jackie and John always visited the children in their rooms.

If the parent-child relationship in the Kennedy family may sometimes have seemed somewhat formal, it was only because of the pressures incumbent on a First Family. Attention and love were given unstintingly; indeed, it is probable that the Kennedys spent more time truly listening to and talking with their children than do average American parents. The moments together were often brief, but they were meaningful.

Along with love went the discipline that Jackie herself exercised in such measure. Only in this way was she able to maintain a private as well as a public life.

Newport Country Club golf pro, Lidner, tells how.

A moment of "unnoticed" shopping is enjoyed in Newport.

Led by member of ballet school, Caroline drags tambourine belonging to classmate, who was pacified when handed another.

First Lady, John, Jr. on lap, drives one-horse cart in Newport, R. I.

Caroline and playmate, Virginia Warner, telephotoed on south lawn of White House.

Leaving Otis AFB Hospital on way to summer home on Squaw Island, Hyannis Port, after giving birth August 7, 1963, to boy who died two days later.

Mother and son, behind shrubbery during formal reception for White House guests.

Leaving Andrews AFB on way to Hyannis Port for Thanksgiving weekend in 1962. John, Jr. was left behind, as in preceding year.

First Lady crouches at head of ramp steps on return from "dream" vacation in Mediterranean.

FIRST WOMAN
FOR THE WORLD

⚜

In a 1955 trip abroad, Jacqueline Kennedy and her husband dined at the U. S. Embassy in Rome. One of the guests was George Bidault, the French Foreign Minister, who found himself engaged in conversation with John Kennedy. An interpreter was needed, and Jackie filled in easily.

Later, she received a short note from Bidault, who, in thanking her for her assistance, remarked that "I have never seen so much wisdom adorned with so much charm." It was but a hint of the admiration people from other lands would shower upon her in the years to come.

Foreigners, almost without exception, took to Jacqueline Kennedy. They were enthralled with her youth and beauty, appreciative of her fluency in languages, surprised at her love and knowledge of the arts, and enchanted with her attention to fashion. She was so startlingly unlike the typical American visitor that she was accepted immediately and sincerely as the most glowing symbol of the "best" of this country. The spark America had been unable to ignite in alien hearts with wealth, warheads, and space achievements, she could kindle with a smile.

This first became evident when she accompanied John Kennedy to Ottawa in mid-May of his first year in office. Relations between the United States and her northern neighbor had been cool during the first days of the Kennedy administration, and this was a crucial visit. Though Mrs. Kennedy certainly did not participate in any discussions involving her husband and Canadian Prime Minister John G. Diefenbaker—who had won office, incidentally, on a platform somewhat antagonistic to the

America's peerless goodwill ambassadress is greeted by Pakistan Rajah, the much bemedaled (with French forces in two wars) Mohammed Walait Khan.

68

With Mrs. Khrushchev at Palais Pallavicini in Vienna, Austria.

At equestrian show in her honor, with chief of Royal Canadian Mounted Police.

United States—she contributed greatly to the improvement of American-Canadian relations.

Like most of the trips that would follow, this one included a state dinner and reception, given by Governor-General Georges Vanier. The following evening, the Kennedys entertained special Canadian guests at the American Embassy. Such events can have striking effect upon national leaders, but they are, by and large, lost upon the general populace, whose glimpse of visiting dignitaries is usually limited to motor caravans and conducted tours. However, Jacqueline Kennedy's presence at such occasions always assured extensive popular coverage by the press.

During her stay, Jackie visited the National Gallery of Art, attended a private display of horsemanship by the Royal Canadian Mounted Police, was interviewed on television in French, and witnessed the Canadian Parliament in session. Her conduct, in every instance,

Accompanied by President de Gaulle of France outside Elysée Palace in Paris.

Kennedys at Versailles Palace.

endeared her to all; indeed, in Commons, the Speaker of the Senate arose and, as she watched, said, "Her charm, vivacity, and grace of mind have captured our hearts."

In three days she had, as one newspaper put it, "revived the good-neighbor policy with a smile and a wave."

This triumph had hardly passed when sophisticated Paris fell before her charms. Parisians had been awaiting her for some time. Almost from John Kennedy's first day in office, Paris publications had found Jackie too fascinating to exclude from their pages. Her French ancestry had something to do with this, but so did her beauty. One French writer put it this way: "Her full lips, high cheekbones, widely spaced, heavily lashed eyes, and black hair all give her an exoticism that emphasizes her strangely toneless and beautiful voice." That a woman such as this should hold a position of importance also thrilled the French. *Paris Match* wrote: "Young, beautiful, rich . . . even Hollywood would never have dared give the role of First Lady to the superb brunette who has captured every heart. She has the look of a star and the silhouette of a mannequin." And, if one wonders what effect the presence of one woman can have upon the image of a nation, the article continues, "Yes, but Americans are more courageous than movie producers. It is really

In gay discussion with Khrushchev during reception at Schönbrunn Palace, Vienna.

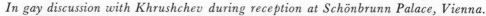

Queen Elizabeth and Prince Philip entertain the Kennedys in June, 1961, marking the first time since 1918 that an American Chief of State and his wife had dined at Buckingham Palace.

During visit to Vienna, Austria, in June of 1961.

Escorted by Canadian Governor-General George P. Vanier to state dinner at Government House in Ottawa.

only in America, whose wonderful people are innocent of envy, that an elegant and beautiful woman could overcome the obstacles encountered in politics." Jacqueline Kennedy was obviously becoming a most precious national resource.

The original purpose of the Paris trip was a meeting between John Kennedy and French President Charles de Gaulle. Relations between the United States and Russia, however, were in a curious state of flux at the time because of our new administration and many old, unsolved problems. When Soviet Premier Nikita Khrushchev proposed a summit meeting with Kennedy at Vienna in early June, Paris became the prelude to that confrontation.

The Kennedys landed at Orly Airport and were met by French President Charles de Gaulle. He had met Jackie the year before in Washington and had been captivated, remarking at the time that if there were anything he might be interested in taking back to France with him, it would be Mrs. Kennedy. His opinion was not changed by the Kennedys in Paris.

A motorcade brought them from the airfield to Paris, past enthusiastic crowds cheering them along the way. As they drove through the Latin Quarter, a group of American students waved a Harvard banner.

The Kennedy-De Gaulle talks began almost immediately. A luncheon break found Jackie Kennedy engaging De Gaulle in a conversation about French history. It was a talk so lively and so detailed that De Gaulle remarked to the President that she knew more about the subject than did most French women. And indeed she did.

She also knew a great deal about Paris, but she had little time to see it as she had on previous trips. Everywhere she went, usually accompanied by Mrs. de Gaulle in a black, bubble-top limousine, she was mobbed by crowds eager for a close-up look.

She would have preferred, as she told reporters, to see Paris on her own, to "walk around and look at the buildings and the streets and sit in the cafés." But Paris was too enthralled by her to permit her any privacy. As one report put it, "It quickly became evident that the radiant First Lady was the Kennedy who really mattered."

This was not lost on John Kennedy. At a luncheon for press correspondents on the last of his three days in the French capital, he introduced himself by saying: "I'm the man who accompanied Jacqueline Kennedy to Paris."

There were two formal occasions during their visit: a state banquet at the Elysée Palace and a dinner and ballet performance at Versailles. For both, Jacqueline Kennedy was thoroughly prepared. Her clothes formed the bulk of some two vanloads of baggage and, though she had been advised to wear American-designed dresses, she boldly chose a Givenchy gown and coat for Versailles. It was a decision that not only further endeared her to the French but, story has it, when John Kennedy, who rarely noticed clothes, saw her that evening, he was somewhat taken aback. "Well," he said, "I'm dazzled."

Right, *First Family of United States and Royal Family of England in official photograph at Buckingham Palace.*

Prime Minister Nehru and Mrs. Kennedy admire ceiling of building called "Rashtrapati Bhavan," residence of British viceroys until 1947, when India became an independent state.

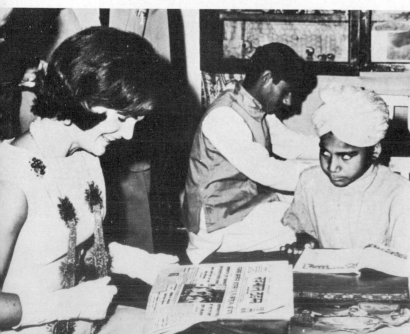

Indian boy steals surreptitious glance in library of Balsahyog children's center, New Delhi.

And well he might have been. Jacqueline had not prepared casually for this trip. Prior to her arrival, a lock of her dark hair had been sent to a leading Parisian hair stylist. He was to change her coiffure several times, creating classical styles especially for the occasion. A top cosmetician was also enlisted to highlight her lovely features. The labors of these artists on a woman of such natural beauty created a picture of femininity that, as far as Parisians were concerned, was unmatched in public life.

There were countless highlights of the Paris trip for Jackie. She visited historical sites—among them, the Empress Josephine's summer retreat at Malmaison—and, in between handshakes that ran to the thousands, she met the one person she had specifically expressed a desire to see. He was André Malraux, the French Minister of Culture, whose novels she had long admired. His sons had been killed in an accident shortly before the Kennedys' arrival, but he attended the state dinner at Elysée Palace. "Mrs. Kennedy was," wrote Arthur Schlesinger, "deeply moved at his appearance, and an enduring friendship began."

The banquet at Versailles was a perfect ending for it all. They dined in the famed Hall of Mirrors and then attended a ballet in the Louis XV theater. It was an experience Jacqueline Kennedy would not forget.

From there, the Kennedys moved on to Vienna. It was a gray, rainy Saturday morning when they arrived and drove to the American Embassy. Discussions between John Kennedy and Nikita Khrushchev began within the hour of arrival. They were not to go well. Laos, West Berlin, a test-ban treaty, and general relations were discussed by the heads of two leading powers of the earth. Khrushchev was unyielding, perhaps to

With Venezuela's President, Romulo Betancourt, for dinner at his residence.

Honored at luncheon given by India's President, Dr. Rajendra Prasad, in New Delhi.

Thousands of Pakistanis line streets of Lahore, throw flower petals, and cheer their President and his beautiful American guest.

show the new and young President that he was a foe not to be taken lightly. John Kennedy was sorely tried during these days as he sought to present reasonable attitudes and to achieve some understanding with his adversary. It was a futile effort.

But the social side of the meeting was more cordial. The Austrians gave their guests a state dinner at Schönbrunn Palace, at which Mrs. Kennedy presented an appearance as enchanting as she had in Paris. Her chief admirer that evening was Khrushchev. The Soviet leader, though firm in his stands during the talks with John Kennedy, was completely taken with the President's wife. They joked easily and at length, she chiding him because he first attempted to impress her with overworked statistics. When the space ventures of both nations were spoken of, Jackie noted that one of the dogs the Russians had orbited around the world had recently had puppies; jokingly she asked the Soviet Premier why he had not sent her one. Two months later, much to the surprise of the Kennedys, he did.

As the talks went on, Jacqueline was not idle. She visited the ancient Spanish Riding School and witnessed a special performance of the famed Lipizzan horses. She toured a porcelain factory and worshiped at St. Stephen's Cathedral, where Franziskus Cardinal Koenig said the mass. It was a particularly impressive ceremony, and the Vienna Boys' Choir made it more so. Jackie was visibly moved.

In Paris, Frenchmen had cried *"Vive Jacqueline!"* as she passed in motorcade. In Vienna she was hailed again—this time, on the balcony of the Pallavicini Palace, where she appeared with Nina Khrushchev. A throng of more than five thousand Austrians cheered the two women, so different in age and appearance. The crowd hailed them both, crying "Nina'" and, not Jacqueline, but "Jackie!" Nina Khrushchev held the hand of her young companion and lifted it high. If the talks between Kennedy and Khrushchev went poorly, the joint appearance of Nina and Jackie showed that human beings can join hands in friendship.

There were few moments as light and gay during the stay in Vienna. One did, however, occur at a luncheon when John Kennedy mentioned to Khrushchev that Jackie thought Soviet Foreign Minister Andrei Gromyko had a nice smile and could be trusted. The Russian leader promptly replied that this might be so, but that Mrs. Kennedy should not forget that many people thought Gromyko also closely resembled Richard Nixon.

78

Opposite, Jackie and sister, Lee Radziwill, ride high during trip to Jaipur, India.

Police hold back newsmen and crowds of admirers as Jackie leaves her London flat on way to lunch with Queen at Buckingham Palace.

Jacqueline Kennedy's observations and appearance influenced the entire European continent, both behind and in front of the "Iron Curtain." A Polish publication, commenting upon the impression she made in Austria, noted that she "has entered the group of a few women in the world who set the style and tone of their epoch . . . This sort of woman has always existed, but never before has her influence been so far-flung or so quickly disseminated. The face and silhouette of Jackie are known to all people over the civilized world."

Official business over, the Kennedys left for London. This was not a state, but a private visit, the purpose of which was to attend the christening of Jackie's niece, Lee Bouvier Radziwill's daughter Anna. They stayed more or less out of public reach at the Radziwills' home but did attend a formal dinner given them at Buckingham Palace by Queen Elizabeth and Prince Philip.

As always, crowds followed them, some three thousand converging on their car and blocking its path as they made their way to the Palace. There, reporters, given a glimpse of the two handsome couples, were at

Jacqueline, flanked by Mexican President Mateos and the President, addresses government officials in Mexico City, disarms them completely by speaking in Spanish.

odds as to who was the more radiant, Jacqueline Kennedy or the Queen. It was of no importance to either of the ladies, however, who found much to talk about. They shared, among other things, a keen interest in horses.

After conversations with British Prime Minister Harold Macmillan, John Kennedy flew back to Washington. Jackie remained in London for two days, shopping mostly for antiques, and then left for a holiday in Greece. She was accompanied by the Radziwills and a government official and his wife. They spent a week touring Athens and cruising among the lovely Greek islands aboard the "North Wind," a 125-foot pleasure yacht owned by wealthy Marcos Nomikos. Nomikos, a member of the Greek Parliament, served as host for their stay.

Touring the Acropolis in Athens with Mrs. Karamanlis, wife of Greek Premier.

Right, watching actors rehearse at the Theater of Epidaurus, in Greece.

Expressing typical tourist reaction to ancient Greek theater in Delphi.

It was a delightful change from the formality of Paris and Vienna. The party enjoyed a performance of Sophocles' *Electra* by the National Theatre at Epidaurus and visited the islands of Delos (birthplace of Apollo), Poros, and Mykonos. Delos was closed to other tourists for the day by the Greek government, while on Mykonos, an island with more than three thousand churches for a population of only five thousand people, every building had been given a fresh coat of whitewash. Jacqueline Kennedy enjoyed herself immensely, even joining in with a group of local dancers at Hydra.

On the mainland, the party stayed at Nomikos' seaside villa outside Athens. And when Jackie went swimming, it all but precipitated a minor naval engagement offshore. A fleet of press photographers in chartered yachts dodged naval patrol boats dispatched to the scene to guard against just such intrusion. A collision actually did occur—a navy boat accidentally ramming into a private yacht—but damage was slight.

The incident was typical, however, of the interest photographers showed in Mrs. Kennedy. They seemed to be everywhere. One might expect this, of course, in Washington, Paris, or London; at airports, along motorcades, or during official receptions. But they sometimes appeared to turn out in even greater numbers when she was enjoying an unofficial visit.

On visit to royal summer palace at Tatoi, near Athens. Left to right: *King Paul, Queen Frederika, Princess Lee Radziwill, Mrs. Kennedy, and Princess Irene.*

Audience with Pope John XXIII, March 11, 1962.

This was especially true in Europe. If she so much as ventured out of doors, in fair weather or foul, shutters clicked merrily in an impressive, if impertinent, salute to her presence. This was just as evident the following year, when she took another European vacation, spending some four weeks at Ravello, twenty miles from Naples. Cameramen photographed her wherever she went and, among other things, recorded her water-skiing in a colorful one-piece bathing suit. If such publicized activities seemed in poor taste for one of her position to a pedestrian few, it also added to the wonder with which the world was rapidly coming to view her. She was obviously a woman who could fill not only many varied, difficult, and enviable roles, but a bathing suit as well.

Caroline accompanied her mother to Ravello and, much to Jacqueline's delight, played happily with the local Italian children. Language was no barrier to her enjoyment.

An earthquake hit Naples during their stay, prompting Mrs. Kennedy to send a message to its victims. It touched Italians deeply, for her words showed true concern for the problems of others. "I am deeply distressed by the destruction caused by the earthquake in southern Italy," she began. "The past two weeks have reaffirmed my admiration and affection for the people of this part of the world and filled me with gratitude for all their kindness and courtesy. That they, who give so much in heart and spirit, should suffer the loss of life and home is truly a calamity. I pray that all who have suffered may speedily be helped in their great need."

After placing a sheaf of white roses at the Gandhi shrine in New Delhi.

87

Earlier that year, in March of 1962, she had been in Italy briefly. It was a stopover, really, on her way to India, but it was not without ceremony. After calling on Italian President Giovanni Gronchi, she had an audience with Pope John XXIII. Their meeting was memorable in that the manner in which it began sheds some light both on the very human qualities of the Pope and the affection in which Jacqueline Kennedy was held everywhere.

Prior to the audience, Pope John had been reminded by his protocol aide that the proper form of address for Mrs. Kennedy was "Madame."

Attending birthday celebration of Crown Prince Sidi Mohammed in Marakesh, Morocco, Mrs. Kennedy witnessed horseback circus as performed by Berber tribesmen.

Right, Jackie gives up privacy to permit press photographers clear shot of her with Caroline and niece, Christina Radziwill, at water's edge in Conca dei Marini, Italy.

Caroline and mother try out water-skiing in Bay of Salerno, Ravello, Italy.

On way to motor launch at Amalfi pier for day of sunshine and swimming.

With Mayor of Amalfi, Galtano Amendola, after attending mass in cathedral.

But, when she entered the room, the elderly Pontiff turned toward her, spontaneously opened his arms, and greeted her warmly as "Jacqueline."

The trip to India had been planned for some time. As far as John Kennedy was concerned, it had been overplanned. He objected to the strenuous itinerary drawn up by Ambassador John Kenneth Galbraith, but, after three cancellations, it finally took place in March. Jackie was to be accompanied by her sister Lee and a detachment of reporters, which, at one time, numbered more than seventy.

Preparations were elaborate, and the Indians were excited over her arrival. Prime Minister Nehru, at whose invitation she had come, greeted her cordially while crowds hailed her as the "Queen of America." Indeed, she received a tour fit for a queen, including a sail down the

Ganges and a visit to the Taj Mahal at Agra, both at sunset and again by moonlight. She rode elephants, observed a snake charmer, witnessed —somewhat reluctantly—a fight between a cobra and a mongoose, visited hospitals, a home for delinquents, and laid a bouquet at the spot where Mahatma Gandhi had been cremated.

It was a full nine days, but another five were to be spent in Pakistan, where she was received with equal enthusiasm by the people and with unsurpassed gallantry by President Ayub Khan. She rode even more elephants, visited the legendary Khyber Pass, and was motorcaded over expensive Afghan carpets.

She finally left with gifts of two tiger cubs from India, a prize bay gelding from Pakistan, and enough brilliant color film so that the United States Information Agency would make a movie of her trip—"Jacqueline Kennedy's Asian Tour." It would be seen on television, released to movie houses, and distributed throughout the world. With a narration by Jackie, it would be a colorful documentary of intense interest to millions.

Visiting world-famous church of St. Panteleone in Ravello, Italy.

First Lady slipped away from police-protected private beach to join other mothers and children at nearby public area.

The price of fame—Mrs. Kennedy, Caroline, and Radziwill niece, on shoulders of friend, out for "quiet" evening stroll in Ravello.

She made other trips during her years in the White House. In December of 1961, she and her husband visited South America, first stopping in Caracas, Venezuela, then Bogota, Colombia. There was some concern at the time over the wisdom of such a visit because, three years before, Vice President Nixon had been subjected to the taunts of hostile crowds and was, for a time, in extreme danger. But John Kennedy was eager to create strong ties between the United States and the more progressive nations in Latin America. Thus, the trip was scheduled.

As it turned out, there was no cause for alarm. The crowds in Caracas were not only friendly but reportedly larger than any ever assembled there for a foreign dignitary. Jackie, once again, proved a decided asset to her husband and her country when she was able to address Venezuelans and Colombians in their own language.

She created a perhaps deeper impression the following year when, in June, she and the President visited Mexico City. Their motorcade from the airport into the city moved at a snail's pace through showers of confetti and friendly cries of *"Viva Kennedy."*

93

In front of the Taj Mahal in Agra, during semi-official visit to India and other Asian countries.

Amidst pomp and colorful pageantry, in carriage with Pakistan President Ayub Khan.

Later, Jackie addressed a television audience in flawless Spanish and then amazed Mexican officials at the National Anthropological Art Museum with her knowledge of the exhibits.

Fluency with languages was not her only attraction. What caught the eye of the women of the world was the manner in which she dressed. Fashion, in the sense of current trends, meant little to her. She wore what she thought appropriate to the occasion and to her and, in so doing, established fashions of her own.

She became, in the words of a leading expert, "the most potent force in international fashion."

Once she entered the White House, her every purchase became newsworthy. Indeed, on her first shopping trip to New York in April of 1961, squads of reporters literally camped in the lobby of the Carlyle Hotel to be on hand when she ventured forth. Every outfit in which she appeared was duly recorded and reported in the press—a plum-colored suit upon arrival, a blue wool dress with alligator shoes for a luncheon, a blue-gray brocade gown for an evening at the City Center Ballet.

The fuss was really staggering. Interest in her clothes was such that she was forced to issue press releases prior to major receptions or trips abroad, detailing her wardrobe. When this was not done before her Asian tour—because she wanted to stress the goodwill importance of the visit and not the fashion aspect—reporters began badgering leading designers, and sometimes their seamstresses, for "inside" information.

What caused this unanimous interest was not necessarily her actual choice of clothes, but more the way in which she chose and wore them. One could, after all, agree or disagree with her selection. There were many who did both. She was not afraid of color, and she preferred simplicity of line. She favored certain designers but was not a woman to be typed. She dressed by no one's standards other than her own. She always had. Even as a young girl, preparing for her debut in society, she spurned the more fashionable shops and selected a dress from a rack in a department store. Her mother was somewhat disappointed, but Jacqueline liked it, and that was that. The only style that interested her was one that was distinctively individual. This, perhaps more than anything, intrigued those who found fashion a topic of importance.

But fashion was only one of her many talents. Wherever she went she brought "charm, vivacity, and grace of mind" that captured all hearts.

On royal yacht for ride up Ganges, Udaipur, India.

Mrs. Kennedy thinks of clothes in the simplest possible terms and shops with purpose, making selections each year from her favorite designers. (See sketches above.) She loves red, especially in a basic tweed suit or evening dress, wears pink and clear yellows, but feels that black can't be overestimated. Disliking "doodads," she prefers good accessories that she keeps for years. Her look is clearly distinctive, and has long led the latest trends.

On her trip to India in 1962, she was acclaimed by the international press (even from behind the Iron Curtain) as the unquestioned leader of fashion in a world that can agree on little else. Below left, Jackie is shown in two of the numerous costumes she wore during this semiofficial tour of the East. Also shown is fashion ad from Leningrad magazine, Mody, spotlighting the "Jackie" look in dress, coiffure, and even in facial characteristics.

THE
ASSASSINATION

❧

*Lyndon B. Johnson is sworn in as 36th President of the United States aboard plane
at Dallas airport, before leaving for Washington.*

It was a day that began with a jest.

John Kennedy, touring Texas in an effort to unite the Democrats of that state, spoke in Fort Worth on the morning of November 22, 1963. Jacqueline Kennedy was not present, and the President noted her absence by saying: "Mrs. Kennedy is busy organizing herself. It takes a little longer, you know, but then she looks so much better than we do."

Later that morning, after the presidential plane, Air Force One, landed at Love Field in Dallas, Jackie looked especially happy. Making her first public appearance since the death of her second son Patrick, she stepped into the sunshine, wearing a trim pink suit with a matching hat set back on her soft dark hair. She wore white gloves and was presented with a bouquet of red roses. The President, in a gray suit, striped shirt, and blue tie, looked fit and in good spirits. They made a handsome couple.

Dallas was giving them an unexpectedly warm reception. Some Kennedy advisers had feared this city, for it harbored many political extremists of the far right who were bitter over the trends in federal government. Four weeks earlier, Ambassador Adlai Stevenson had been spat upon and hit over the head with a sign by a group of angry hecklers in protest of a speech he had made supporting the United Nations. Handbills denouncing the President had been circulated, and on the day of his arrival, a full-page newspaper advertisement harshly challenged his loyalty to the Constitution.

But, as a city of growing wealth and importance, Dallas could not be omitted from a tour of Texas. Besides, John Kennedy would not shy

One of the last pictures taken prior to assassination.

Mrs. Kennedy instinctively leaps on trunk of car, seeking help after fatal shots.

from threats. According to historian Arthur Schlesinger, Jr., he even discussed with his wife and an aide before leaving Fort Worth that day the impossibility of preventing a determined assassination attempt.

The crowds, however, were large and friendly. They cheered loudly as the President and First Lady, sharing a limousine with Governor John Connally and his wife, passed in motorcade through the city. Mrs. Connally turned to the President and remarked on the spontaneous warmth of the reception as their car moved down a slight grade past the Texas School Book Depository.

High in that building waited Lee Harvey Oswald, a twenty-four-year-old misfit, the father of two small children by his Russian wife. He held a rifle and he was ready. In just seconds, he fired.

What followed has since been recorded in great detail, but to most it will always remain as blurred as the photographs of the event taken by amateur cameramen at the roadside. The fact was that John Fitzgerald Kennedy had been mortally wounded. He would be pronounced dead at Parkland Memorial Hospital at approximately 1 P.M., but his life actually left him there on the highway in his wife's arms. The world would think of little else for four days.

Jacqueline Kennedy's initial ordeal did not end until after four o'clock the following morning. She stayed at her husband's side almost constantly—in the hospital, on the flight back to Andrews Air Force Base in Maryland, in an ambulance to Bethesda Naval Hospital where the body was prepared for burial, and finally back to the White House where, in the East Room, she knelt by his casket, her pink suit still stained with his blood.

Earlier, aboard the plane at Love Field, she had witnessed the swearing in of Lyndon Baines Johnson as the thirty-sixth President of the United States. And, sometime during that day, she had taken off her wedding ring and placed it in her husband's hand. It was but one of the many moving gestures she would make to mark forever this most painful of human tragedies.

State and military funerals in Washington are conducted by a special military command. Their procedures are firmly established by tradition, the personnel well drilled in their duties. Honor guards are provided, six matched gray horses pull the caisson, which is followed by another steed, saddled but unmounted, with the boots reversed in the stirrups. It is all well established. But John Fitzgerald Kennedy's burial would call for many special arrangements, coordinated by his brother-in-law, Sargent Shriver, in consultation with Jacqueline Kennedy.

Among the requests she made was that her husband's coffin rest upon the catafalque that, close to a century before, had borne the body of Abraham Lincoln. It was done.

Just weeks before, Kennedy had enjoyed a performance at the White House by bagpipers from the Black Watch Scottish Highland Regiment. His wife asked that they take part in the funeral. They did.

Jacqueline Kennedy, her clothing blood-stained, helped by Attorney General Robert Kennedy, as she debarks from plane that carried the late President's body back from Dallas.

On a trip to Ireland, the President had been most impressed by a drill team from the Military College. His wife felt their presence would be appropriate. They came.

She thought, too, of the grief of others. On Sunday, she asked Robert Kennedy to relay her sympathy to the wife of the Dallas policeman, J. D. Tippitt, who had been slain while attempting to apprehend Oswald. She showed concern, also, for those who had been close to John Kennedy, and, as a mother, she was, of course, deeply concerned about the effect his death would have on his children—especially Caroline. She had always believed they should be aware of the events taking place around them. Now she wanted them to be present at the events that would mark the passing of their father. And, dressed in blue coats, they were there on Sunday when the body was moved from the White House to the Rotunda in the Capitol, and on Monday at St. Matthew's Cathedral.

Construction on 17th Street is used as vantage point to watch funeral procession led by John F. Kennedy's widow and his brothers on way to St. Matthew's Cathedral.

More than a quarter of a million people passed the President's casket during the hours it lay in the Rotunda. Jacqueline Kennedy came many times. She was there first at noon on Sunday when, with Caroline, she knelt and kissed the flag that draped the coffin. And she came again that evening with Robert Kennedy. Later, she walked out into the night, passing close by the long line of those who waited to pay their respects. A woman recognized her and tears came to her eyes. Jacqueline Kennedy embraced her silently.

Monday dawned clear and, shortly before noon, Jacqueline, with Robert and Edward Kennedy at her side, led a procession from the Capitol to the cathedral. Behind them came a remarkable gathering of world leaders, including eight heads of state and ten prime ministers. There were two hundred and twenty in all, representing some ninety-two nations and five international bodies. It was an assemblage unique in modern history.

Cardinal Cushing conducted the requiem mass, and Luigi Vepi sang "Ave Maria," as he had ten years before at the wedding of Jacqueline Bouvier and John Kennedy. Eleven hundred people attended the services.

Jacqueline took her children in hand as the coffin was led from the church. On the steps she stood firm and straight as it was placed on the caisson. Caroline fought back tears, while John, whose third birthday this was, raised his hand in salute.

Right, "With the deepest expression of grief."

There was more to the tragic day—the long procession to Arlington, which passed more than a million mourners, the services at the grave site in the slanting rays of the afternoon sun, the sharp report of a rifle salute, the lighting of the eternal flame, the folding of the flag . . . taps.

But Jacqueline Kennedy's day was not yet over. After her husband's body was lowered into the ground some thirty minutes past three, she returned to the White House, where, in private, she received President Eamon de Valera of Ireland, President de Gaulle of France, and Emperor Haile Selassie of Ethiopia. The latter had visited Washington just two months before. Mrs. Kennedy had still been mourning the death of her second son, Patrick, but had made a special effort to greet the tiny monarch.

She then greeted guests on a formal receiving line. She had shed tears just twice during the day.

Body of late President, John Fitzgerald Kennedy, is lowered into its grave at Arlington Cemetery, November 25, 1963.

One can only imagine the torment that must have been hers. In the words of novelist Katherine Anne Porter: "She stared with dawning anger in her eyes, in the set of her mouth, yet with the deepest expression of grief I have ever seen, a total anguish of desolation, but proud, severe, implacable."

The world marveled at her conduct. Miss Porter wrote: "No one who witnessed that three-day funeral service, in presence or by screen, can ever say again that we, as a nation, cannot properly conduct the ceremonies of our state. We have been well taught."

Even if Jacqueline Kennedy had done nothing before or since, this last parting would have been enough. She honored her husband's bright promise, gave substance and meaning to the senselessness of his death, and brought glory to the country he loved.

No one could have done more.

AFTER THE ASSASSINATION: PUBLIC LIFE

❧

A year of mourning was announced.

Nonetheless, Jacqueline Kennedy could not pass from public view. Her every moment was considered newsworthy enough to be followed by the press, not only in the United States but abroad. Whether taking her children Christmas shopping in Palm Beach or skiing in Vermont, reporters and photographers were ever present and did not hesitate to violate her privacy. Their endless pursuit, however, was no more than a reflection of intense public interest.

Thousands upon thousands of messages of sympathy were sent to Mrs. Kennedy by a saddened public. She wanted each one to be acknowledged, but the volume was such that it was impossible without aid, both physical and financial. Congress appropriated the sum of $50,000 to ease the task, while volunteer workers established offices in the old State Department Building. Each letter was opened, read, a return envelope addressed, and a letter of acknowledgement, bordered in black, inserted and mailed. It was a mammoth job, and the former First Lady was grateful to those who helped her, often visiting their busy offices.

In January, she appeared on television to publicly thank the American people for their interest, and to promise that no letter would go unanswered. She dressed simply, in black, and spoke softly but with feeling. "The knowledge of the affection in which my husband was held by all of you," she said, "has sustained me, and the warmth of these tributes is something I shall never forget. Whenever I can bear to, I read them. All his bright light gone from the world. All of you who have written to me know how much we all loved him, and that he returned that love in full measure. It is my greatest wish that all of these letters be acknowledged. They will be, but it will take a long time to do so, and I know that you will understand.

"Each and every message is to be treasured, not only for my children but so that future generations will know how much our country and people in other nations thought of him. Your letters will be placed with his papers in the library to be erected in his memory along the Charles River, in Boston, Massachusetts. I hope that, in years to come, many of you and your children will be able to visit the Kennedy Library. It will be, we hope, not only a memorial to President Kennedy but a living center for young people and scholars from all over the world.

Entering General Assembly Hall of United Nations with U. S. Ambassador, Adlai Stevenson, to attend annual U. N. concert in December, 1964.

"May I thank you again on behalf of my children and of the President's family for the comfort your letters brought to all of us. Thank you."

Eventually, close to one million messages were received and answered.

Her name was also affixed that year to thousands of cards thanking contributors to the John Fitzgerald Kennedy Library in Boston. Originally, John Kennedy had planned to establish a presidential library at Harvard after completing his days in the White House. He had had no firm design for the future, but had felt that such a place could serve not only as the repository of his private and official papers but as a base of operations, so to speak, from which he could write, perhaps teach, or even return to politics.

Upon his death, plans were made to create a memorial library, and the Kennedys, rather than solicit a few large contributions, sought

With Mrs. Lyndon Johnson and Robert Kennedy at reception in 1964.

Ireland's President, Eamon de Valera, bids farewell after calling on former First Lady at her Washington residence.

Mrs. John F. Kennedy at luncheon given by U. N. Secretary-General, U Thant, in honor of Edgar G. Faure, former Premier of France.

Escorted to pew by Richard Cardinal Cushing, who celebrated solemn pontifical requiem mass for the late President in Boston.

the help of all people so that it would truly be a public memorial. Each donation was acknowledged by Jacqueline with these words: "The President's family and I wish to express our deep appreciation for your contribution to the John Fitzgerald Kennedy Library. The reality of this library will serve as a perpetual memorial to the President, and we are grateful for your support."

A devoted populace contributed more than ten million dollars in less than a year's time.

Jacqueline's acknowledgements of funds and messages were, because of the enormous volume, in printed form. And, though certainly treasured by those who received them, they could not approach the value that was being placed in early 1964 upon her actual signature. A

West Berlin Mayor, Willy Brandt, visits Jacqueline in Washington.

Attending premier of "The Eleanor Roosevelt Story" with Franklin D. Roosevelt, Jr.

Mrs. Kennedy at exhibit of Indian painting during one of her rare public appearances of the year.

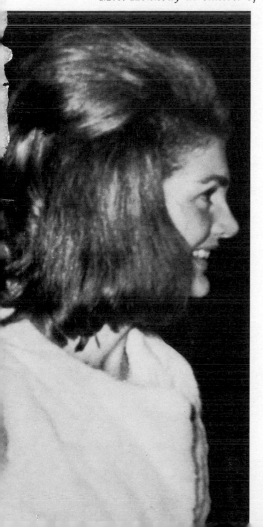

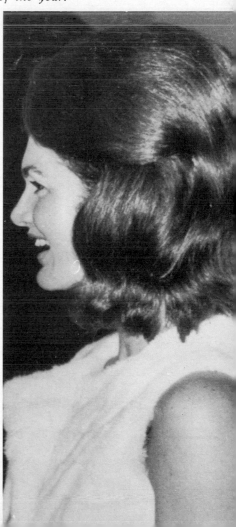

letter she had once written to a man in England—he had read of the Kennedys' wealth and had asked for money—brought $3,000 at an auction in New York. It was the highest sum then paid for a letter written by a living American woman. As other long-forgotten letters, many of no consequence, appeared for sale, Jacqueline became concerned and attempted to discourage such tasteless commercialization. There was, however, little she could do to halt it.

A similar stir was created over her first social appearance in 1964. Though it was an impromptu dinner at a private club, it received wide coverage in the press, which emphasized that one of the guests was the well-known movie actor, Marlon Brando. As recorded, the reporters considered it an inappropriate choice because Brando, an enormously talented actor, is best remembered for his more primitive portrayals. As a matter of fact, neither had a hand in the arrangements, such as they were. Film producer George Englund, who was connected with a Kennedy charity, had been invited by Lee Radziwill to Jacqueline's residence. It was an informal occasion, and it seemed not unnatural that Brando, who was working with Englund at the time, accompany him. After a brief talk, dinner was mentioned and Jacqueline was asked if she would care to join them. She did, but it was something of a mistake. Reporters quickly learned of their presence at the club, and the incident made headlines the next day.

From that day, the attempts of the press to link her name with various men have not ceased. Movie magazines picked up the theme immediately, and her face appeared on the covers of many. There was no substance to these reports; indeed, many were positively absurd, one even hinting that she might eventually wed an actor who once admitted during an interview that he admired the Kennedys and was also interested in a political career. If this seemed flimsy enough ground on which to base a romance, the publication then compounded its sin by admitting that Jacqueline had never met the actor in question.

But such situations cannot be avoided in a free society. Neither could Jacqueline Kennedy avoid the attempts of others to plan her life. Some felt she should enter politics—it was even mentioned that she should seek the Vice Presidential nomination in 1964, while early in 1966, a group in New Jersey, where she had purchased an estate, suggested that she would make an ideal candidate for the Senate. Ambassadorships were mentioned, while others sought to persuade her to write a syndicated newspaper column or to appear regularly on television.

She would have none of this.

Public life was behind her, at least for the time being. She did, however, take an interest in the political aspirations of former presidential press secretary, Pierre Salinger. He sought the Democratic Party nomination for Senator in California and entered the primary. After seeking the approval of Robert Kennedy, Jacqueline consented to an interview with a California newsman. Salinger had based his campaign on his close relationship with John Kennedy, and Jacqueline backed him, saying that her husband "valued his advice and counsel on all major matters." Salinger won the nomination, but was eventually defeated in the election.

Jacqueline played no other part in the hectic political events of 1964. She did not even participate in the campaign of her brother-in-law, Robert Kennedy, for a Senate seat in New York, though with her son John she did visit his headquarters.

She did not appear at the convention hall that year in Atlantic City, but she was much in the delegates' minds when Robert Kennedy rose to present a film tribute to his late brother.

For sixteen minutes delegates stood on their feet and hailed the brother of the late President. Their cheers were warm, their applause constant, their tears spontaneous. It was a roaring tribute, a din of love and respect. But when Robert Kennedy spoke, the crowd was hushed.

With Jacqueline Kennedy on her right, Queen Elizabeth of England presents an acre of historic English ground to the American people in memory of John F. Kennedy. Location is Runnymede, site of the signing of the Magna Carta in 1215.

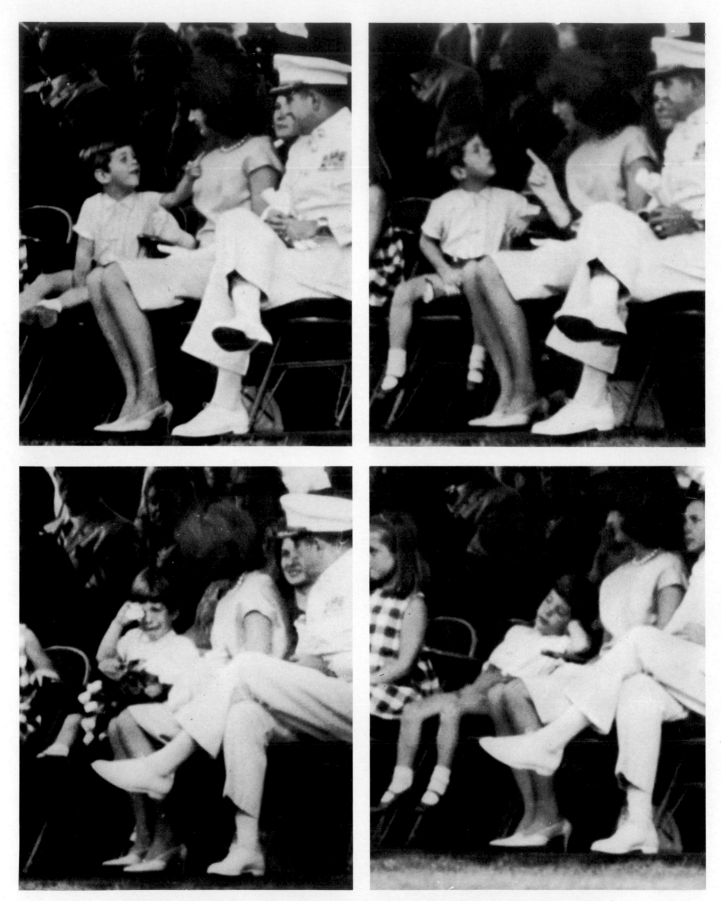

116

During traditional Sunset Parade ceremonies at U. S. Naval Base in Brooklyn, John Kennedy, Jr., like any other 4-year-old, got restless. Advised by his mother to behave, his feelings are deeply hurt, bottom left. *Tired of it all,* bottom right, *he falls asleep.*

Dear Mrs Johnson —

I just heard you were going to be in town today and wondered if you would like to listen to the Debate with us —

I'm having a Listening Party at 1028 Connecticut Ave and would love it if you came and brought anyone you like —

But I expect you are exhausted from your travels (I loved your story in N.Y. Herald Tribune) and are looking forward to relaxing + watching TV at home — If so. I understand perfectly!

As always
Jackie.

At request of Mrs. Lyndon Johnson, letter received by her from Mrs. Kennedy in 1960 was withdrawn from auction. The correspondence was expected to bring $1,000.

The film, comprised largely of newsreel clips, traced the bright career of John Kennedy, but the scenes with the greatest impact were those with his wife and children. When the narration of these scenes quoted a few lines from a song the President had loved, the country— for millions also watched on television—felt its sorrow surge anew. Those words expressed it all: "Ask every person if he's heard the story . . . and tell it strong and clear if he has not . . . that once there was a fleeting wisp of glory . . . called Camelot."

On the final day of the convention, Jacqueline sat quietly at a reception given for her by the Averell Harrimans, attended by some six thousand guests, and listened to the special kind of tribute to her husband she had arranged. John Kennedy's favorite poem, "I Have a Rendezvous With Death," by Alan Seeger, and several other selections were read by Fredric March and Florence Eldridge. When Jacqueline addressed those assembled, she was visibly touched, her words brief: "Thank all of you for coming—all of you who helped President Kennedy in 1960. May his light always shine in all parts of the world."

There was considerable speculation about Jacqueline Kennedy's plans once her year of mourning was over. Gloria Steinem, in an article for *Esquire* magazine, quoted a State Department official as saying: "This November 22nd, when her retirement is over, Jackie could become, if she wanted to, the most powerful woman in the world." She

Assisted in removal of evening coat upon arrival at Mark Hellinger Theater for opening of "On a Clear Day You Can See Forever."

would not choose to. However, she did not retire completely from public life. In addition to being a member of the board of the Whitney Museum of American Art, the John F. Kennedy Center for the Performing Arts, and the John Fitzgerald Kennedy Memorial Library, she is also honorary chairman of many other organizations and foundations.

Her social life was restricted mainly to attending opera, concerts, art exhibits. Her range of escorts was wide—the late Adlai Stevenson for a concert at the United Nations, producer Harold Clurman for an evening at the theater. And, late in 1965, she entertained.

The occasion was a party in honor of John Kenneth Galbraith, the former Ambassador to India, who had been responsible for her Asian tour three years before. Previously, at private dinners, the guest lists included noted writers, artists, and members of the Kennedy family. Now many of the same guests assembled at her Fifth Avenue home in New York City. From there, they went on to view an art exhibit—to which Jackie had lent a number of paintings—and then to an exclusive restaurant, reserved for the evening. It was a successful return to the role of hostess, and Jacqueline was, as always, beautifully dressed, this time in a white crepe sheath topped by a sleeveless mink shell. Later that week, in Boston, she took part in the Golden Trumpet Ball for the benefit of the Boston Symphony Orchestra.

Whatever she had been through, she had not lost her taste for excellence. As for her impact on the public at large, the American Institute of Public Opinion, otherwise known as the Gallup poll, established her as the most admired woman in the world.

She had not only survived her ordeal but had grown in stature, not only in the eyes of the public, but privately as well. "She's not," noted one of her acquaintances, "the brittle flower some of us thought she was."

If some still mused about her future, the question could only be in the direction it would take. Wherever that might be, the world knew she would go only as she always had—proudly and with purpose.

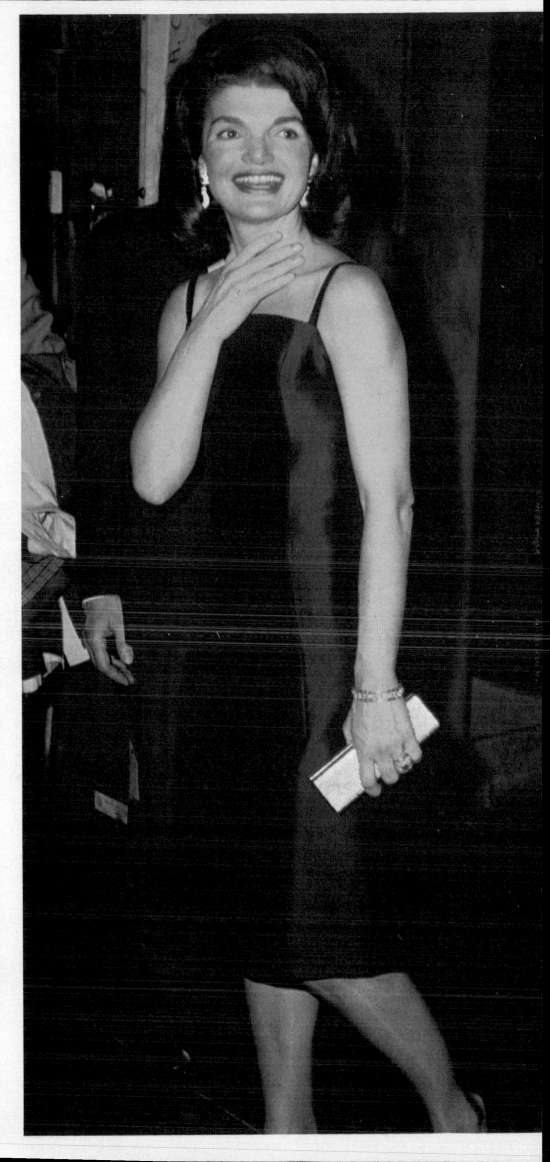

Backstage after the performance.

Alan J. Lerner, of "My Fair Lady" fame, who escorted Mrs. Kennedy, was author and producer.

AFTER THE ASSASSINATION: PRIVATE LIFE

❧

The nation and the world shared her sorrow, the sorrow of that November day, but none could fill the emptiness.

"When I go on a trip," she revealed to a national magazine, "it's all right, but it's so empty and depressing to come home."

There were many who sought to help her, among them Robert Kennedy. He had been at her side as the casket was lowered and placed in an ambulance at Andrews Air Force Base, and he was at her side often in the days, weeks, and months that followed. She once said that he was the member of her husband's family for whom she would "put my hand in the fire," and now the bond was even stronger. All the Kennedys, for that matter, would remain close to her, and this was important because she had raised her children to be a part of that family. But it would not be enough, nor would the city of Washington, which she had grown to cherish.

At first, she intended to stay on in the capital. The Averell Harrimans had given her the use of their house in Georgetown after she had moved from the White House, and she eventually purchased a home nearby. But the city held too many memories, and the curiosity of tourists became oppressive. They came in droves, standing outside her house for hours waiting for a glimpse of her and the children. If their privacy had been restricted both before and during their stay in the White House, now it was even more so. Determined, as she had always been, not to lose it altogether, she decided to leave Washington.

After leaving White House, Mrs. Kennedy moved into Georgetown home (right) of Averell Harriman. A few weeks later, she purchased a twelve-room house (far right) across street.

120

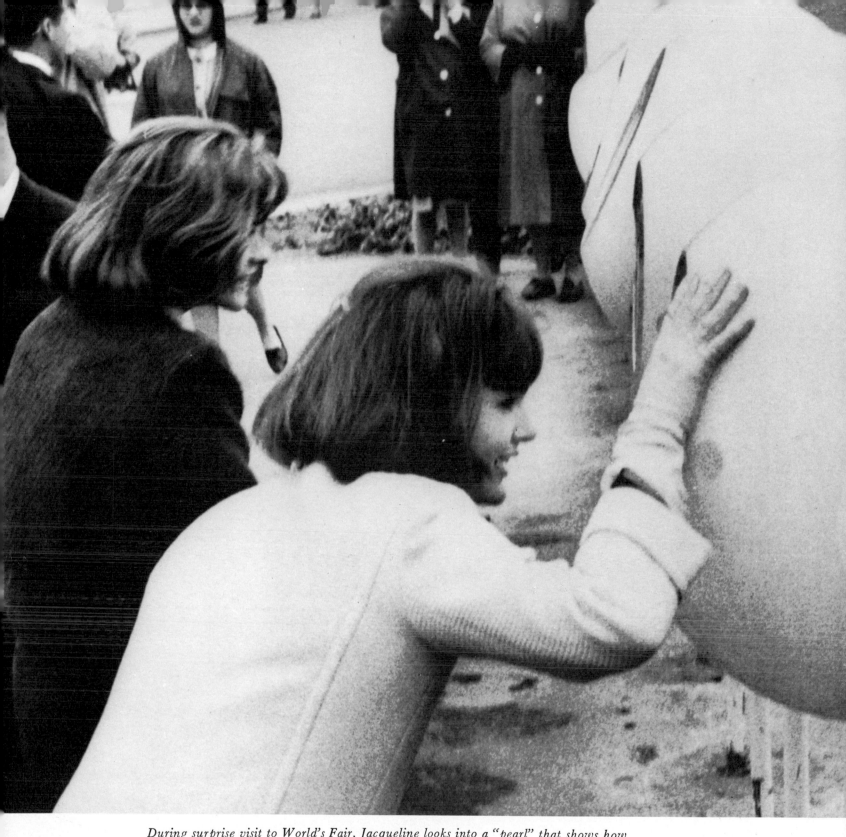

During surprise visit to World's Fair, Jacqueline looks into a "pearl" that shows how she would look as a blonde. She apparently is amused.

At hospital, right, to visit injured brother-in-law, Senator Ted Kennedy, who was hurt in plane crash. Far right, mother and daughter approach Harriman-loaned home with high hopes.

This could not have been an easy decision, for it took her away from Arlington. She had been there often since the burial, having returned the very night of the funeral with Robert Kennedy and the next day with Caroline. Her two deceased children had been placed alongside their father in December of 1963, and she had fresh flowers placed on the graves each week. Still, Washington had become too great a trial, so she put it behind her.

Her sister Lee urged her to settle in New York City, the very largeness of which affords a certain anonymity to the individual. After

Left, Jacqueline and Caroline at New York World's Fair.

Mother and children on the bridle path in 1962. It was discovered in June of 1964 that Caroline, at time picture was taken, had fallen from her famous pony Macaroni, breaking "a couple of small bones" in her left wrist.

receiving assurances that steps would be taken by the city to insure her privacy, she purchased an apartment on Fifth Avenue, not far from the Metropolitan Museum of Art.

New Yorkers did, to a large degree, respect her wishes. Once she ventured to take the children for a rowboat ride in Central Park, but gone were the days when she might dare to take them trick-or-treating, as she had done when they were in the White House.

The move, however, did not change her way of life to any great extent. Holidays and vacations were often spent with other members of the Kennedy family—at Palm Beach, Hyannis Port, or various ski resorts. This was not just a ritual for her, or a longing for the past, but a conscious effort to see that her children remained part of the Kennedy clan, as the press so often called it. The closeness of the family was somewhat alien to her own background, but it was something she admired and found of value.

Once, when Caroline had fallen and tears had come into her eyes, her mother told her, "Kennedys don't cry." Remaining a part of that large family reinforced such teachings. Kennedys do cry, of course, but when they are together, it is a large, active family with little time for tears.

Robert Kennedy had this in mind when Jacqueline's thirty-fifth birthday approached in 1964. It would be the first one she would celebrate since the death of her husband. A private dinner had been scheduled at a fashionable New York restaurant for purposes of advancing

A skiing holiday at Aspen, Colorado, was enjoyed by the entire family in December of 1964.

124

The young widow returns from European vacation, suntanned and rested, destination unknown.

Changing of Buckingham Palace Guard is "reviewed" by Kennedy children and cousin, Anthony Radziwill.

Richard Cardinal Cushing on his seventieth birthday receives kiss from John, Jr.

the Kennedy Memorial Library and, though it did so, it also turned out to be a surprise party for Jackie, complete with birthday cake and presents.

Quiet moments with her family and friends, however, were not always so spontaneous. They had to be planned, for public interest in her affairs remained high. In an effort to find privacy, she rented an estate in Glen Cove, Long Island, and later purchased another home in New Jersey so that she and the children could enjoy holidays away from the crush of the curious. It was an ample estate, near Peapack, and gave her an opportunity to ride once again. Caroline was developing into as fine a horsewoman as her mother and grandmother had been, and even John-John, who at first had shunned horses to ride wth his father in helicopters, learned to ride.

Travel was considered part of the children's education, as well, but among its difficulties was the unending publicity. In early 1966, a skiing vacation in Switzerland proved so irresistible to photographers that the first day turned into a mass of confusion. The Kennedys never did get to ski. Jacqueline solved this the following morning when she and the children posed for twenty minutes of pictures before taking to the slopes. The procedure, though no doubt resented by Jackie, would establish a pattern; perhaps the only one by which she and her children could get through life. The fact is, neither the press nor the public wanted to forget the wife and children of John F. Kennedy.

Nor did Jacqueline Kennedy want them to forget. Just before leaving the White House after her husband's death, Mrs. Kennedy, shattering precedent, had the following inscription placed on the mantel in their bedroom: "In this room lived John Fitzgerald Kennedy with his wife Jacqueline during the two years, ten months, and two days he was President of the United States."

Estate in Glen Cove, L. I., leased by Jacqueline Kennedy for week-end use. Mrs. Kennedy purchased, in late 1965, property in Peapack, New Jersey.

125

Building on New York's Fifth Avenue in which Mrs. Kennedy purchased apartment in July, 1964.

Two years, ten months, and two days. Arthur Schlesinger would round it off to "A Thousand Days," in a remarkable record of the brief administration of John Kennedy. No matter how it was counted, it would always remain in the minds of men as too short.

For Jacqueline Kennedy, that time had been longer—ten years, two months, and nine days of marriage, a year or so longer of courtship. It had begun when she was barely twenty-four years of age, and it was over just five months past her thirty-fourth birthday.

She was keenly aware of that ending. "Jack was something special," she was quoted as saying, "and I knew he saw something special in me, too. The years in the White House were really the happiest time for us, the closest, and now it's all gone."

At christening, in New York's St. Patrick's Cathedral, of Robert Kennedy's ninth child, Matthew Maxwell Taylor Kennedy.

First Woman for the World, and of the world, leads Leprechaun, Caroline's new pony, into ring at 4-H Horse Show in Osterville, Mass., during summer of 1965.

At another time she said: "I should have known that it was asking too much that I might have grown old with him, and see our children grow up together."

This was important to her. She told Theodore Sorenson: "I think the major role of the First Lady is to take care of the President . . . [but] if you bungle raising your children I don't think whatever else you do well matters very much."

At the prime of her life she would have to go about the task alone. Could the years she had with her husband sustain her through the private and public ordeals she still had to face? The world will not cease to wonder.

Jacqueline Bouvier was born into wealth and reared with propriety. Her background was not typical of the people she would eventually come to represent, but she would become their finest feminine symbol. And, after the tragedy of her husband's death, their most poignant reminder of the promise of this land.

"She came among us like some wildly unexpected fairy queen, and with her goes the heart of everyone who lived in this place when she did."

But those thousand days have long been over. Jacqueline Kennedy has assumed a place apart and above that of the widow of a deeply mourned leader. She is more than a former First Lady. She is a woman of, and for, the world.